Stains/water damage noted.

— MJ @ GVK 10/6/18

The

BIG BOOK OF LIONEL

THE COMPLETE GUIDE TO OWNING AND RUNNING AMERICA'S FAVORITE TOY TRAINS

ROBERT SCHLEICHER

MBI

This edition first published in 2004 by Motorbooks International, an imprint of MBI Publishing Company, Galtier Plaza, Suite 200, 380 Jackson Street, St. Paul, MN 55101-3885 USA

Motorbooks International titles are also available at discounts in bulk quantity for industrial or sales-promotional use. For details write to Special Sales Manager at Motorbooks International Wholesalers & Distributors, Galtier Plaza, Suite 200, 380 Jackson Street, St. Paul, MN 55101-3885 USA.

ISBN 0-7603-1826-3

Acquisitions editor: Dennis Pernu
Edited by Amy Glaser
Layout by LeAnn Kuhlmann

Printed in China

On the front cover: You can recreate 1955 with a Lionel Union Pacific 4-6-6-4 articulated steam locomotive and a lash-up of GP-7 and GP-9 diesels like these on Robert Babas' layout.

On the frontispiece: Four action accessories are featured in the industrial park on Richard Kughn's layout, including three coal-loading accessories. The red and green structure in the foreground is the 497 Coaling Station, the beige structure with a red roof is the 97 Coaling Station with chain-belt-buckets to hoist the coal into the tower, and the angled gray conveyor of the 397 Coal Loader is just visible behind it. The green, yellow, and red accessory is the Lionel Log Loader.

On the title pages: The bridge piers on Larry LaJambe's layout were cut from 2"x4"s, sanded, and painted. The ridge is a combination of several Lionel plate girder bridges that were cut and cemented end-to-end, upside down.

On the back cover 1: The news agent in the Lionel 128 Newsstand happily hands a newspaper to his customer. The apartment buildings on Richard Kughn's layout are Korber Models kits.

On the back cover 2: Hobby shops carry a variety of model railroad paint you can use to touch-up chipped areas. Floquil Box Car Red was a good match for the brown on this caboose.

About the Author: Robert Schleicher of Niwot, Colorado, is a veteran hobby industry writer and publisher, and the author of several MBI titles, most recently *101 Projects for Your Model Railroad, The Big Book of Model Railroad Track Plans,* and *Slot Car Bible.*

CONTENTS

PART I

Building
A Lionel Layout

Modern Lionel trains operate around the classic reproduction of the O Gauge tinplate No. 128 Illuminated Station and Terrace on Richard Kughn's Lionel layout.

Chapter 1

LIONEL TRAINS, 100 YEARS OF FUN

To most Americans, Lionel means toy trains. Generations of people remember Lionel toy trains from their childhood and have passed that joy onto their children or grandchildren for over 100 years. Few icons in America have the status of Lionel, with a life span longer even than Harley-Davidson or Ford Motor Company. Buy a Lionel train and you own a piece of history.

THE VALUE OF LIONEL TRAINS

Lionel Trains are unique among model railroads and toy trains because the entire spectrum from toy to hobby to collectible is encompassed among Lionel toy train products.

Lionel is the simplest of all toy trains to operate because everything snaps together easily and runs reliably. Lionel trains run equally well on wood floors, carpets, and tabletops, which is not true of the smaller HO or N scale trains.

Lionel offers a full range of products including trains that are replicas of the toys of the 1940s and 1950s, semi-scale models that look just like their original counterparts, and exact scale models that are precise replicas of real cars and locomotives. You can run, collect, or use them as the basis for an exciting model railroad. Some Lionel fans enjoy all three aspects of the hobby.

What sets Lionel trains apart from the smaller HO and N scale trains is the heft and bulk of the models. When a Lionel locomotive rolls down the track, you can hear the rumble, and in many cases, you can actually feel the vibration as the massive model moves along.

Since Lionel only keeps products in the line for a few years, it can introduce an incredible array of new products each year to replace discontinued models,

You can recreate 1955 with Lionel's Union Pacific 4-6-6-4 articulated steam locomotive and a lash-up of GP-7 and GP-9 diesels like these on Robert Babas' layout.

Some permanent Lionel model railroads, like Larry LaJambe's walk-in layout, have spectacular scenery.

The rock canyon extends all the way to the floor for walk-in access to Larry LaJambe's layout.

which often reappear a few seasons later with new road numbers and other updated enhancements. This constant flow of new products means that you can obtain a Lionel replica of your favorite real locomotive or freight car or passenger car, especially if you are willing to wait for your favorite item to join (or rejoin) the Lionel line.

RELIABLE RAILROADING

Lionel trains are designed to run better, and be more reliable, than any other model trains. Real railroads have two rails, but Lionel has three, and the rails are oversized so that it's easier to create complex track layouts without the special electrical gaps in the rails or intricate wiring required with two-rail systems. The larger rails allow you to run your trains on just about any surface—even on the carpet—without derailing.

Lionel prides itself on producing products that provide easy-to-master operation, even if that operation includes running 12 trains at the same time with remote-controlled signals, switches, and cars being loaded and

These are two of the many bridges on the spectacular Lionel Visitors Center layout.

unloaded all at the push of a button. Today, toy makers are fond of saying that their systems are "plug and play." Lionel was one of the first companies ever to use create plug-and-play toys, which have developed into a very user-friendly system.

Lionel's TrainMaster Command Control system allows you to run almost as many trains as you wish, each under completely independent control. You can uncouple most locomotives anywhere you desire and operate dozens of remote-controlled accessories to load and unload the cars all at the same time. You can even automate a series of train manuevers on or off the mainline and over whatever routes you select.

Every O or O-27 train Lionel has ever made will operate on any Lionel track. Some O Gauge and Standard O locomotives require a minimum 31- or 54-inch circle, but the track gauge is the same for all Lionel O products.

You can choose the simple transformer that came with the train set or add it to the TrainMaster Command Control system and still be able to operate any locomotive made for O-27, O, or 0-72 track. There is no such thing as an obsolete Lionel locomotive, car, or accessory. The tinplate Lionel toys from the 1930s will operate right alongside the newest models.

It's likely that Lionel trains travel a greater number of miles per model than any HO or N scale train. They can be counted on to run when you want them to, and they will continue to run for many miles and years. If a train does break or wear out, replacement parts and service are available from the nearest authorized U.S. Lionel service stations. The concept of "keep them running, no matter how many miles or how old" is one of the unspoken policies that has kept Lionel in business for over a century.

In 2002, Lionel created the Phantom III locomotive and articulated passenger cars as a fantasy series of what artists imagined trains of the future would look like.

Lionel produces very limited runs of some interesting locomotives, like this Pennsylvania Railroad 6-4-4-6 articulated, becoming instant collector items.

THE MEANING OF MINIATURE

All models or miniatures are designed in proportion to the real thing. With models, the term proportion is usually replaced with the word *scale*. Most Lionel products are O scale, which is 1/48 the size of the real trains. The common HO scale trains are 1/87 scale. Most Lionel trains are a bit smaller than precise O scale because they were deliberately designed to operate in compact spaces. You can set up a Lionel O Gauge layout in less space than you could put an HO scale layout.

The least expensive (and smallest) Lionel products are designated as O-27 size, and the slightly larger models are usually called O Gauge. In some Lionel catalogs, the medium-sized models are referred to as O Gauge, Traditional Line, or Postwar Celebration Series trains. O-27 models have often been included in "entry level" (popular priced) train sets for 50 years. Cars and locomotives in the Postwar series are O Gauge models that were first introduced in the late 1940s, 1950s, and 1960s, and are popular with adult hobbyists because they harken back to their own childhood and the times they shared with their first Lionel train set. The newest models are called Standard O or Scale and are nearly exact reproductions of the earlier models with improved dimensions, performance, features, paint, and lettering.

EXACT SCALE TRAINS

These Standard O Lionel models that are precise 1/48 scale are the largest Lionel steam and diesel locomotives. Because of their longer wheelbases, they can only be operated on 54-inch-diameter curves and 0-72 switches (sometimes called turnouts). These larger Standard O models will often derail on tighter O Gauge curves. To accommodate those who love the largest prototype models of the Iron Horse, Lionel offers *near-scale* models of a number of truly massive locomotives. The LionMaster series features cleverly engineered large wheelbase engines that operate on the 31-inch curves and O Gauge switches.

Two Lionel stamped-steel Bascule Bridges span the entrance to a small harbor in Richard Kughn's layout.

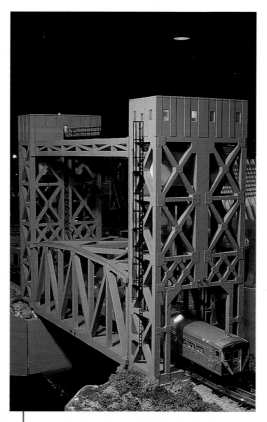

The Operating Lift Bridge on Richard Kughn's layout is one of the largest models Lionel has ever produced.

Five remote-control levers are used to operate the Lionel Intermodal Crane, on Richard Kughn's layout.

Most of the track on Richard Kughn's layout is assembled from 72-inch diameter curves and 0-72 switches, and is ballasted for more realism.

The Prewar era 700E Lionel O Scale New York Central Hudson is perhaps the most famous Lionel steam locomotive, but the new (and slightly smaller) LionMaster model has better performance, and the new Hudson has TrainMaster Command Control.

OTHER THAN O SCALE

Lionel has also produced models in other scales throughout most of its history. In the 1930s, the most expensive toy trains were massive models, even larger than O scale, called Standard Gauge. The distance, or gauge, between the rails for O scale is 1 1/4 inches, but these huge Standard Gauge toys operated on track with a gauge of 2 1/4 inches between the rails. Why Lionel elected to name their exact-proportion O scale trains "Standard O" has been lost in the Lionel lore of the past four decades. Just try not to confuse Standard O with the more massive Standard Gauge Lionel trains. Lionel has, and will continue to, introduce replicas of the stamped-steel tin-plated Standard Gauge cars, locomotives, and accessories from time to time. If you see the two gauges next to each other, you will never mistake one for the other.

Today, Lionel also has Large Scale models in G gauge, which is 1 3/4 inches between the rails. Frankly, G gauge is the most confusing scale in the entire hobby, because the models built to run on G gauge track vary from as small as 1/32 to 1/24 scale. Large Scale is unique in that it is designed to run indoors or outdoors. Lionel has offered Thomas the Tank Engine models and a series of 1/24 scale narrow gauge locomotives and cars that run on G gauge track. Lionel has also offered a Large Scale 4-4-2 Atlantic; EMD GP-7, GP-9, and GP-20 diesels; a boxcar; a gondola; a flatcar; and a caboose to run on Large Scale track. These models are all about 1/32 scale. Today, models like an operating Christmas holiday handcar and a boxcar with digitally reproduced Christmas carols make up the Lionel Large Scale category.

Lionel also produces HO scale models, and offers a select array of diecast metal Command Controlled steam locomotives and diesel engines with digital sound and smoke, but they are beyond the scope of this book. It all began prior to World War II when Lionel offered a locomotive, some cars, and track in OO scale (1/72 scale, slightly larger than HO scale), but they were never reproduced for mass distribution.

A small, but stalwart, group of OO enthusiasts formed over the past 50 years and continually petitions Lionel to reproduce these classic pieces of the past. No decision has been made to bring these classics back to life at the time of this printing.

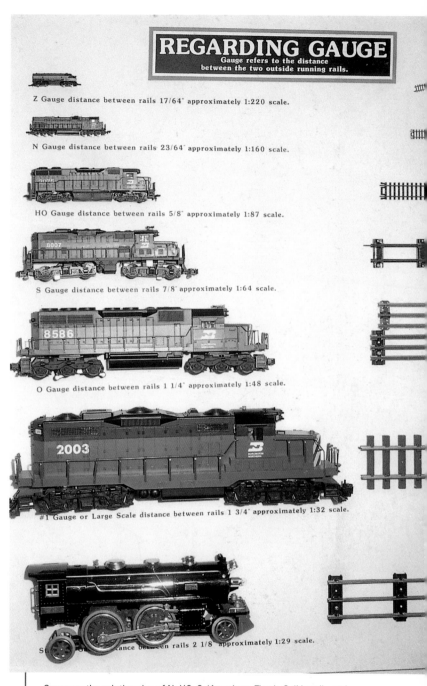

REGARDING GAUGE
Gauge refers to the distance between the two outside running rails.

Z Gauge distance between rails 17/64" approximately 1:220 scale.

N Gauge distance between rails 23/64" approximately 1:160 scale.

HO Gauge distance between rails 5/8" approximately 1:87 scale.

S Gauge distance between rails 7/8" approximately 1:64 scale.

O Gauge distance between rails 1 1/4" approximately 1:48 scale.

#1 Gauge or Large Scale distance between rails 1 3/4" approximately 1:32 scale.

Standard Gauge distance between rails 2 1/8" approximately 1:29 scale.

Compare the relative size of N, HO, S (American Flyer), O (Lionel), and Large Scale (Lionel) diesels, along with a standard Gauge Steamer, on this display at the Lionel Visitors Center.

From left to right American Flyer two rail track, Lionel O gauge track, and Lionel FasTrack. FasTrack combines realistic detail with the operating simplicity of three-rail track.

The American Flyer bay-window caboose with cupola is an unusual car, and Lionel has offered it in a variety of road names. This original car is from the 1950s.

AMERICAN FLYER

Lionel purchased the American Flyer S scale product line in 1966. Each year, Lionel offers a range of new American Flyer cars, locomotives, and accessories to run on original American Flyer two-rail track (which is still plentiful in the secondary U.S. marketplace). The S scale models are 1/64 scale and a bit smaller than Lionel's own O-27 cars and locomotives. The American Flyer models, however, are all exact scale.

Lionel has offered "resurrections" of most of the original American Flyer diesel locomotives, freight cars, and accessories to accommodate a growing hobbyist segment who consider American Flyer's gauge the perfect scale. Many Lionel dealers also offer used American Flyer locomotives, cars, and track to round out the product line.

LIONEL CLASSICS

Toy trains produced before World War II were constructed mostly of stamped steel. Collectors refer to these early toy trains as "tin plate" because the steel was plated with tin to minimize rust. These trains were often painted in bright colors with a high gloss enamel—a characteristic that is still common today.

More recently, Lionel has produced a variety of stamped-steel replicas of the locomotives, cars, and accessories from the 1920s and 1930s. These resurrections have been referred to as Lionel Classics or Lionel Standard Gauge. These are almost exact re-creations of the plated-steel products Lionel originally produced in the early twentieth century. The Lionel direct resurrections of classic products are marked and most have minor changes to distinguish them from the more valuable originals.

One of the most famous toy trains was Lionel's replica of one of the first streamlined trains, the 1934 Union Pacific M10000 articulated passenger train. Lionel introduced the model the same year the real train began operation.

Lionel has also reproduced the American Flyer GP-7 in several paint schemes. This Union Pacific GP-7 is an American Flyer model from the 1950s.

Lionel has offered the classic American Flyer lightweight corrugated-side passenger cars in Santa Fe, *California Zephyr*, and C & O lettering as well as Union Pacific, Missouri Pacific, Northern Pacific, New Haven, New York Central and Southern Pacific paint schemes. These are original American Flyer cars from the 1950s.

This 2-4-2 is a stamped-steel locomotive from 1941 with a fan-operated electric motor whistle in the tender. The 2-4-2 locomotive had a visible reversing-unit lever in front of the cab.

Entry-level Lionel train sets of the 1940s had four-wheel cars like this 804 Shell tank car, 809 Manual Dump Car, and 807 caboose, all from 1939. These models have never been reproduced.

Perhaps the most interesting Lionel Classic replica is the Hell Gate double-track bridge in green and white, like this one on Richard Kughn's layout.

LOCATING LIONEL PRODUCTS

You can locate your nearest authorized Lionel dealer through Lionel's website at www.lionel.com or by phone at (800) 454-6635. Lionel introduces hundreds of new items each year and retires just as many. Only items like track, accessories, and transformers are likely to remain the same year after year. Lionel does make new production runs of its most popular locomotives, freight cars, passenger cars, and accessories, but the re-creations will have different paint and markings to preserve the collectablity of every Lionel products old and new.

Very few of the Lionel products you will see in this book are currently in production as shown. A few of the more recent items may still be available from authorized Lionel dealers, but you might have to look for them at a dealer that sells new and used Lionel equipment or search for them at train meets, flea markets, garage sales, or on eBay.

I strongly encourage you to have your dealer send you Lionel catalogs when they are published every January and August so you will know which items are being introduced so you can reserve your favorite selections with your dealer before they are available. As you become familiar with certain Lionel line "regulars" (locomotives, cars, and accessories that often return to the product line with new livery in each successive catalog), you can best choose what items you need for your particular collection or layout. Your Lionel dealer can also special-order one of several books that illustrates and describes virtually every train product Lionel has ever built.

MODERN MAGIC

The wonder of Lionel in the new century is that the trains are more versatile and fun than before. Lionel still offers a series of recreations of the toys of the 1940s and 1950s and introduces brand-new ones each year. Lionel also offers a growing series of exact-scale models that are larger and as detailed as HO model-railroad products. You have a choice of toy trains or exact-scale model railroad locomotives and cars, including massive articulated steam locomotives, replicas of 6,000-horsepower modern diesels, exact-scale freight cars—and all of it will operate reliably on three-rail Lionel track.

The O Gauge 814 Automobile/Furniture boxcar was produced in 1932. The Lionel Classics line has offered reproductions of similar O Gauge and Standard Gauge tinplate models.

All Lionel models from the 1930s have sparkling paint and plating like this 804 Shell tank car.

Lionel's O scale diesels have cab interiors, metal details, fan-driven smoke, and built-in TrainMaster Command Control, like these scale replicas of the Alco FA-2 diesels.

Lionel's diesels included the most modern machines, such as this Burlington Northern EMD SD70MAC and Union Pacific General Electric Dash 9-44CW.

Chapter 2

WHERE TO PUT YOUR LIONEL LAYOUT

Some lucky model railroaders have cavernous basements they can fill with a model railroad. Others of us that lack space are lucky to find part of a spare bedroom for our Lionel layout. The good news is that you can create a layout in a space as small as 4x6 1/2 feet, fill a basement, or have a temporary layout on the floor of the living room.

FINDING FLOOR SPACE

If you're looking for the space to assemble a Lionel layout on the floor, try to find an area that does not have much traffic. If you normally eat your meals at the kitchen table, perhaps the dining room could be condemned for a railroad right of way, or you may be able to use part of the living room or a portion of the den. A

This double-track layout fills out a 4x6 1/2-foot tabletop with room to operate two trains.

There's space around a Christmas tree for an inside loop of 42-inch diameter track and an outside loop of 54-inch diameter track.

Lionel layout can certainly encircle a home theater without bothering anyone. Perhaps half of a two-car garage might be available, especially in the summer.

PERMANENT LAYOUTS

Layouts at the Lionel Visitors Center and at the homes of Richard Kughn, Robert Babas, and Michael Ulewicz are built with tables that are strong enough to walk on. All of these layouts also have permanent track with real ballast and scenery shaped from Styrofoam and plaster.

RAILROADING IN THE BEDROOM

There is enough room on a double bed for a Lionel layout. If the bed is mounted high enough, the layout can be built on a table that can be slid beneath the bed when not in use, and placed on the bed or on separate legs above the bed when it's time to operate your trains.

A 4x6 1/2-foot layout, like many of the layouts in Chapter 3, will fit on a bed and can include a two-level loop-t loop layout. You can expand any of the 4x6 1/2-foot plans shown in Chapter 3 onto a 5x9-foot Ping-Pong table if you use the 0-72 switches and no tighter than 42-inch diameter curves. This will allow you to operate most exact-scale Lionel locomotives and cars. If you want to run the largest articulated steam locomotives, you'll need at least a 9x12-foot table for the plans that use 0-72 switches and 72-inch diameter curves.

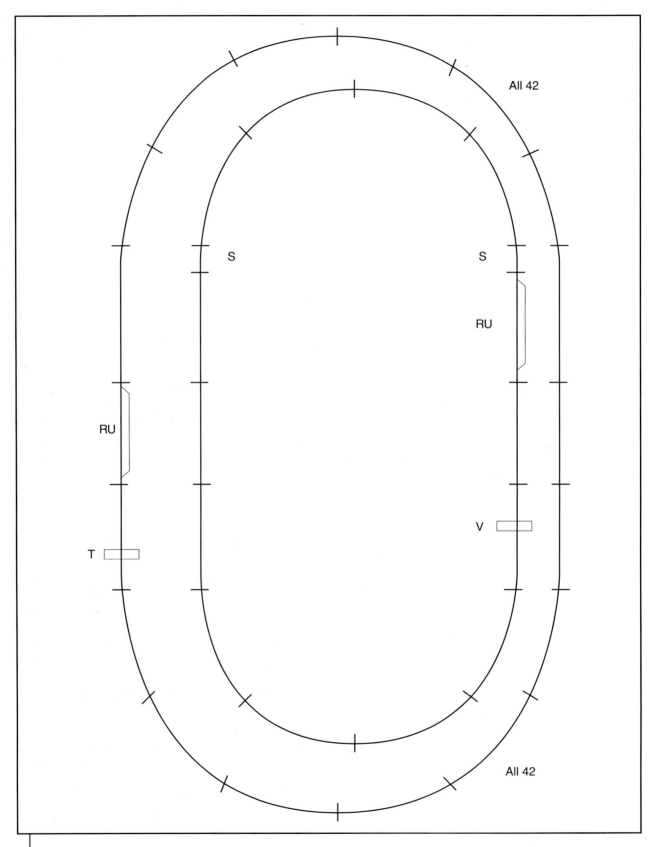

All 42

S

S

RU

RU

V

T

All 42

This simple double-track oval requires just 4x6 1/2-feet. The short lengths of track "S" are optional. The "RU" indicates the best location for an uncoupling track or remote control track, and the "T" and "V" are locations for Lockons, or terminal tracks.

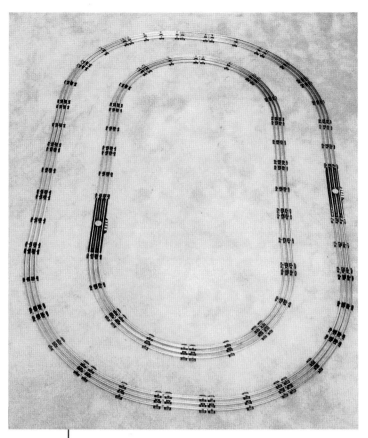

The double-track plan expanded with half-length straights in the outer 42-inch diameter oval makes it possible to install double crossover pairs of switches as shown in Chapter 3.

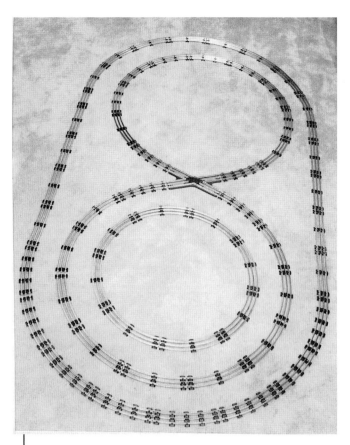

Three trains can be operated in a 5x9-foot area, each with its own transformer for independent control or with TrainMaster Command Control.

These track plans are drawn for O Gauge track, but you can assemble most of them with O-27 track or with Lionel FasTrack. The O-27 layouts require about 10 percent less space, and the FasTrack layouts will require a few more inches of space. The numbers on the curves indicate the diameter of the track sections. All straights are standard length unless half sections or smaller segments are indicated.

LAYOUTS FOR A DOUBLE BED

The 4x6 1/2-foot dimension may seem odd, but 4 feet is the standard width of a variety of construction panels, and the length is just short enough to tuck under a double bed. There is enough room for a double-track oval with 31- or 36-inch-diameter curves on the inside track and 42-inch-diameter curves on the outside track and straights three tracks long. If you offset the inside oval, there should be enough room for a pair of O Gauge or O-36 switches to make a crossover for operations like those described in Chapter 7.

If you add a pair of half-length straights to each of the 42-inch curves, the straight sections will be spaced far enough apart so you can put a pair of O Gauge switches on both sides of the layout. The two pairs of crossovers allow trains to travel from the inside oval to the outside oval without backing up.

Any of these plans can be expanded to fill a 5x9-foot Ping-Pong table or a 20x20-foot room. Conversely, you can select just one element of each plan for your layout. The figure 8 will fit on a 4x8-foot panel.

LAYOUTS FOR 5 X 9 FEET

This layout will allow you to operate three trains at once with three separate power packs for independent control of each train, or you can opt for a single PowerMaster system. All but the very largest Lionel steam locomotives will operate on the 42-inch curves of the figure 8 or on the 54-inch curves of the outer oval. Only the smaller wheelbase locomotives and cars or LionMaster products will operate on the 31-inch circle. If you don't know the

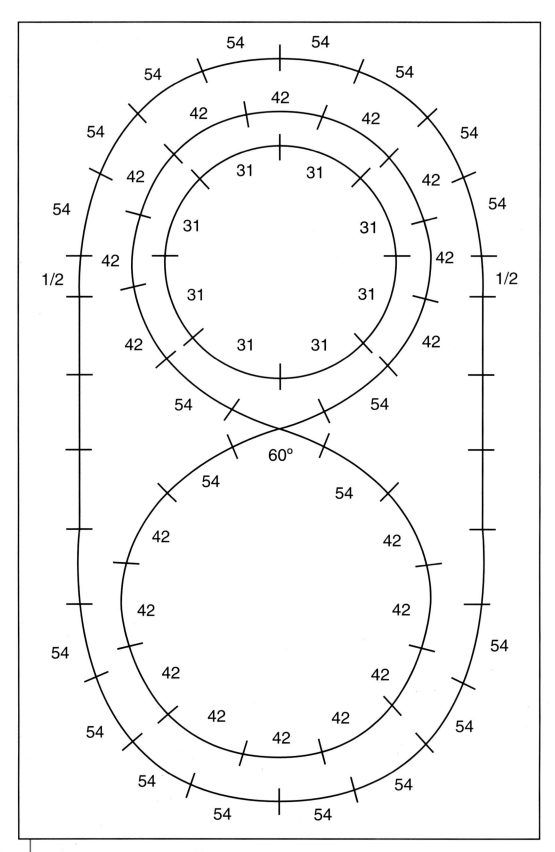

The outer oval is a simple design with 54-inch diameter curves to fill the 9-foot length of the tabletop. The figure 8 includes four pieces of 54-inch diameter curves to have proper alignment with the 45-degree crossing.

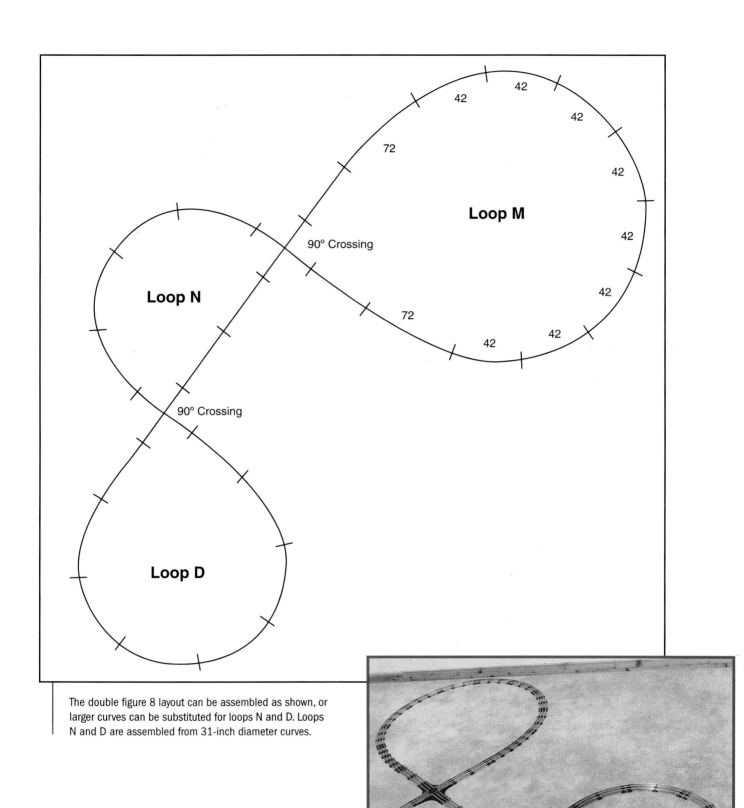

The double figure 8 layout can be assembled as shown, or larger curves can be substituted for loops N and D. Loops N and D are assembled from 31-inch diameter curves.

This double figure 8 is a great layout to begin with on the floor. At Christmas, the tree can be placed in either loop. The Loop M is assembled with 42-inch diameter curves and two 72-inch diameter curves to align the track with the 90-degree crossing.

This on-the-floor Lionel layout was designed to operate two trains as described in Chapter 7. The freight is parked and waits for the passenger train to come rattling across the two 90-degree crossings. The figures at the crossing are Disney characters. The round black-and-white object is an on-off switch to "park" the train. Note that the O 27 and O tracks are combined.

This is an expanded on-the-floor layout with a convoluted double-8 mainline and an industrial siding. In the upper right, there are two yard sidings to "park" two trains, while the third train circles the mainline. The two yard tracks actually extend beneath the couch.

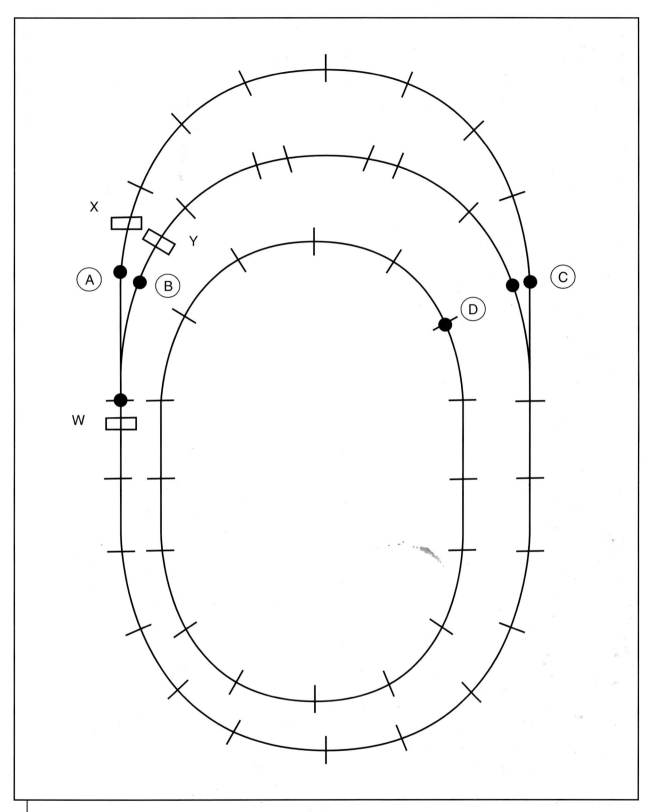

The 72-inch diameter switches can be used with smaller curves. Note, however, that one piece of 42-inch diameter curved track and four pieces of 54-inch diameter curved track are needed, along with two custom-cut 4-inch straights for the inner passing siding on this particular layout.

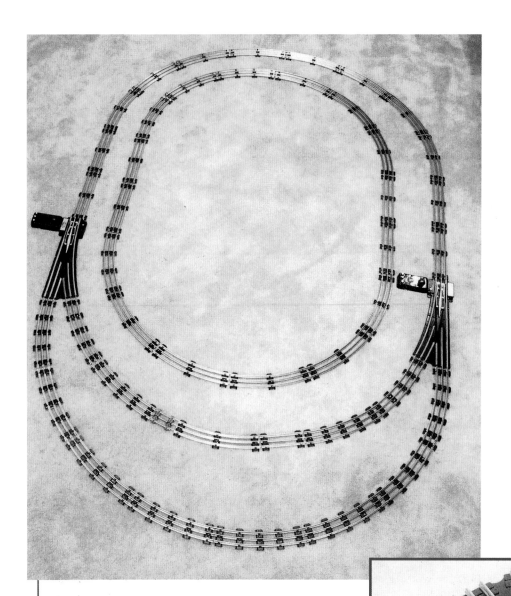

This 4 1/2x7 1/2-foot layout is large enough to allow almost any Lionel scale locomotive to operate. The inner oval uses 42-inch diameter curves and the outer oval uses 54-inch diameter curves with 72-inch diameter switches.

Lionel sometimes refers to the 0-72 switch as a 72 curved-path switch because the curved path is a 72-inch diameter curve large enough to accommodate the longest O Scale Lionel steam locomotive. I recommend using these switches wherever possible because they are much more realistic than the 0-31 (O Gauge) switches.

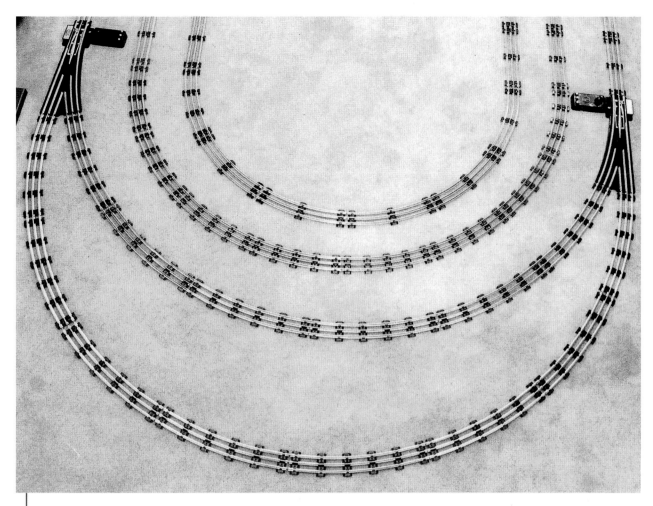

If you have the room (and you just might if you build the layout on the floor), use 72-inch diameter curves for the outer oval. This layout can accommodate four trains, one each on the two inner ovals and two on the outer oval with passing siding.

minimum diameter curves a locomotive will negotiate, please refer to the information in the catalog and on the product packages.

The double figure 8 can be assembled on a Ping-Pong table. It was the basic layout design I started with for the two different layouts on the living room floor. When you are laying track on the floor, you don't have to worry as much about space, but it can be easier to start with a plan that you know will work and expand it.

EXPANDING TRACK PLANS TO FILL THE SPACE

Every layout in this book can be expanded indefinitely in either width or length. Most of the plans are designed to compress as much track as possible in a minimum space, so you cannot usually make them smaller, but making them larger is no problem. With the double figure 8 plan, I wanted to be able to use both 42- and 31-inch curves with Lionel O Gauge track. If you are operating larger locomotives, you may need to use

42-inch or larger curves. Loop M on the plan can be duplicated in place of Loop D, and 42-inch curves can be used for Loop N. If you need to operate the largest Lionel locomotives or if you just have plenty of space, you can use 72-inch curves by adapting some of the 9x12-foot plans from Chapter 4.

The trick to expanding track plans is to insert matched pairs of straights on opposite sides of the layout. The ovals for 4x6 1/2-feet have three straights. If you add pairs of straights to each side, the plans can be expanded to 4x7 1/2-feet. If you want to fill a 4x8-foot panel, add additional pairs of half-length straights.

You can replace a 31-inch curve with a O Gauge switch or you can replace a standard-length straight with an O Gauge switch. I replaced some of the O Gauge curves on the double-figure 8 layout on my living room floor with switches to create a passing siding. Similarly, if you are using O-27 track, you can replace the O-27 curves or straights with an O-27 switch. You can also

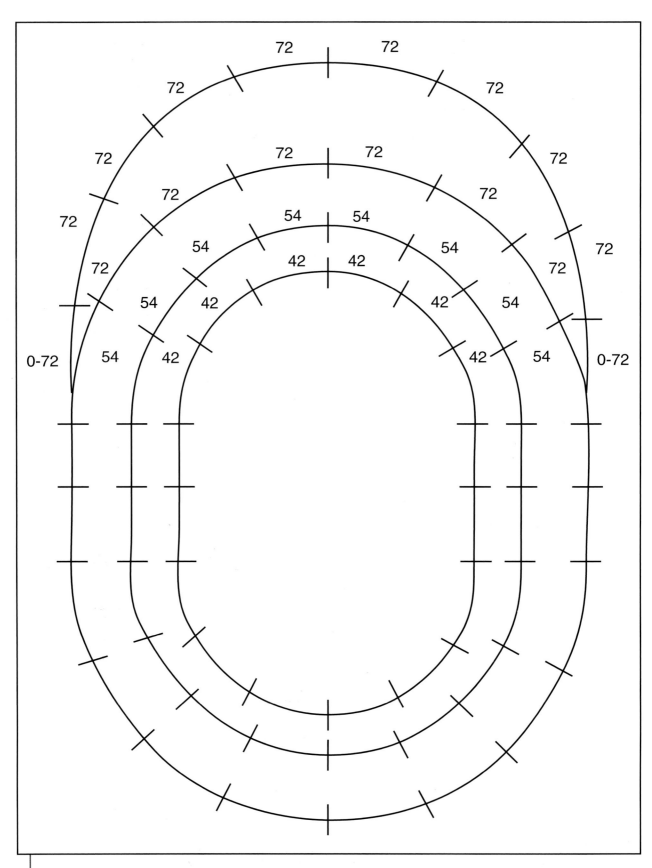

72 72 72 72 72 72 72 72 72 72 72 72 72 72 72

72 72 54 54 72 72 54 54 42 42 54 54 42 42 42 42 54 54 42 42

0-72 54 42 42 54 0-72

This plan requires a minimum of 6x9 feet, but it will accommodate even the largest Lionel steam locomotives on the outer oval.

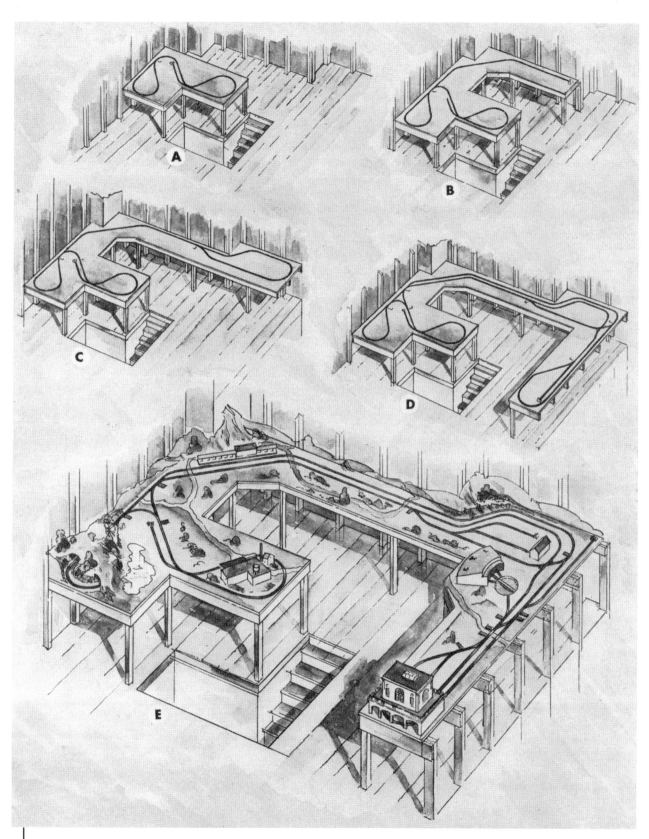

This is a delightful way to expand an 8x8-foot layout into about 12x20 feet. This type of layout design is called a walk-around or shelf because you can walk around beside the trains, and the narrow shelf provides easy access for any derailed trains. *The Model Builder's Handbook, courtesy Lionel LLC*

Oh yes, 20x20 feet is much better than a Ping-Pong tabletop. Robert Babas allocated plenty of tabletop space for the Lionel layout in his basement.

replace an O-27 42-inch curve with an O-27 42-inch curved-path switch. There are no 42-inch switches for O Gauge track, however. There are 0-72 switches for O Gauge track, so you can replace a 72-inch curve on any plan with a 0-72 switch.

With FasTrack, which is 0-36, you can make the same replacements. However, because it boasts several additional track diameters and switch configurations (0-36, 0-48, 0-60, 0-72), you have more options.

THE REALISM OF LARGE-RADIUS CURVES

A few of the very largest Lionel steam locomotives require a minimum 72-inch diameter curve. They will derail on anything smaller. If you want to operate these locomotives with switches, you'll also need to use the 0-72 switches. Most of the Lionel O scale steam locomotives require at least a 42-inch minimum curve and some require 54-inch curves. Since there are no 42- or 54-inch O Gauge curves, you'll need to use the 0-72 switches for these locomotives. I have included several track plans in Chapter 3 that utilize 0-72 switches, even though some of the curves may be as sharp as 42 inches.

Honestly, 72-inch switches are much more realistic than 31- or 36-inch switches, which are actually about as tight as those that trolleys used to negotiate street corners. Even the long extruded aluminum Lionel passenger cars look more realistic on the 72-inch curves. This track plan would allow four trains to operate, one each on the two inner ovals and two on the outer oval with a passing siding. I would encourage you to use 0-72 switches whenever possible, especially if space is not an issue.

This 4 1/2x7 1/2-foot double-track O or 0-27 Gauge layout can provide operations for three trains, one on the inner oval and two on the outer oval (described in Chapter 7). The inner oval has 42-inch curves, the outer oval has 54-inch curves with a single 42-inch on the inner track and a pair of 4-inch-long filler pieces of track that must be cut to fit (described in Chapter 5). This can be accomplished with FasTrack using 36-inch curves on the inner oval and 42-inch curves on the outer oval.

If you have a space that's 6x9 feet, you can assemble an oval with 72-inch switches and 72-inch curves to operate the largest locomotives Lionel has ever made.

Any of these plans can be expanded to fill a basement. Richard Kughn's layout has a double-track oval running around the perimeter of the island table with a half-dozen alternate routes on the inside of the table. Derailed trains can be reached by walking across the sturdy tabletop.

Remember, any of these layouts can be expanded in any direction. This one could be expanded to run on a shelf around the walls of a 9 1/2x13 1/2-foot room, with a duck-under at the entrance like the double-track layout in Chapter 3.

EXPANDING YOUR MODEL RAILROAD

You can start with a Lionel layout as small as 4x6 1/2 feet and expand it to fill a basement, garage, or attic. The drawings provide an example of a layout in an attic that begins at about 8x8 feet (A). The layout table is extended into an 8x16 foot area, and the inside area of the room is left for the operators to walk beside the trains (B). The layout is expanded again to about 12x18 feet to include a reverse loop (C). The layout is kept on a relatively narrow shelf so derailed trains can be reached without having to walk across the tabletop.

The final expansion runs the layout down the third wall (D) to fill the 12x18-foot space and still leave room for the operators to walk beside the trains. Additional sidings, industries, a passenger terminal, and scenery are added to the final version (E).

This type of model railroad is called an around-the-wall or shelf layout. Larry LaJambe's layout has a walk-in access aisle disguised as a deep canyon. All of the other Lionel layouts in this book are built on a large tabletop. Richard Kughn's and the Lionel Visitors Center's layout are island-style, layouts which allow access to most derailed trains by walking around the outside of the layout. Access to the remote parts of Robert Babas' or Michael Ulewicz's layouts is only possible by climbing up on the table and walking gingerly across to reach derailed trains. It is possible to have hidden access hatches to reach the trains. Richard Ulewicz has a couple on his layout.

Builders note: Always assume trains will derail in the places that are hardest to reach. Plan access hatches throughout your layout to reach these places.

The pleasure of seeing the trains in action on their own tabletop world is worth the time and effort it takes to construct a layout table.

Chapter 3

TRACK PLANS FOR THE FLOOR

Lionel layouts have been assembled on the floors of attics, basements, living rooms, garages, dens, and dining rooms for over a century. Lionel has designed its track to be strong enough to be assembled on bare wood, concrete, or carpet. The new FasTrack track system was designed to be almost as tough as the traditional all-steel Lionel track, with the added benefit of providing its own realistic and stabilizing road bed.

ON-THE-FLOOR LAYOUT—YOUR FIRST CHOICE?

There are advantages to both on-the-floor and tabletop layouts. When the layout is on the floor it can fill the room, run around table legs, and travel into other rooms. The floor-level layout really seems to be going some-where; in a way, it's more realistic than a tabletop layout with mountains and tunnels. The on-the-floor layout maintains a toy-like aspect that is a joy to behold and play with. If you are planning an on-the-floor layout, you

After the presents are unwrapped, consider expanding the layout into the room with a figure 8, and just to provide interest, a peanut-shaped oval.

There's just enough room around the Christmas tree for one 31-inch diameter and one 42-inch diameter oval.

This double-track mainline requires just 4x6 1/2-feet of floor space.

To make sure each track joint stays tight, slide a track clip below each joint. This is the Lionel O 27 Track Clip.

should use FasTrack. No other track allows your trains to run as smoothly on uneven surfaces.

Often, you can create far more complex layouts on the floor because you do not have to be concerned about reaching derailed trains. If a train derails, just step over the tracks and rerail it. On a tabletop layout, you need to provide walk-in access or build the table strong enough to walk on so you can reach the derailed trains on the distant parts of the layout. Also, you can test possible permanent track plans on the floor before you build them into a layout.

SECURING TRACK-TO-TRACK

With O and 0-27 Gauges, each Lionel track joint is designed for a firm press fit. Eventually, however, the vibration of the heavy locomotives can loosen the track joints, especially if the layout is assembled on a carpeted floor. If just one or two track joints seem to loosen more often than others, you can tighten the offending joints with pliers using the techniques in Chapter 5.

To keep the track joints tight, install one of the Lionel O-27 track clips across the bottom of the ties at each track joint to keep the tracks firmly connected. Lionel also offers an O Gauge track clip. One of the advantages of FasTrack is that it utilizes both pin-to-rail connections and plastic ball-and-socket connections. FasTrack will not loosen up with use.

TRACK PLANS FOR LIONEL

All of the plans in this book are marked with the sizes of any curved or straight track sections that are larger than the standard O Gauge, O-27, or 0-36 FasTrack curves and straights. On this plan, the 42-inch curves are indicated, as are the few half-length or smaller straight track sections.

The letters "RU" indicate places to install remote-control tracks or uncoupling tracks. Some of the layouts also have circled letters to indicate where to install the fiber pins in the center rail to divide the layout into electrically isolated blocks so you can operate two trains as described in Chapter 7.

OVAL WITH REVERSE CUT-OFF

As suggested earlier, Lionel trains look more realistic on larger curves, and you should use the largest curve you can fit in the space available. This oval with a reverse loop cut-off track and a single siding uses mostly 42-inch curves because there's room for them in a 4-foot-wide area. The reverse cutoff is a good layout style because it allows you to reverse the direction of the trains on the track. Trains traveling counterclockwise around the oval will need to back through the reverse cutoff to change directions. Trains traveling clockwise can head through the reverse cutoff to change direction.

OVAL WITH FIGURE 8

At a glance, this compact plan looks like a figure 8 combined with an oval. It will fit in just 3x6 1/2-feet because it uses all O Gauge curves and switches. The plan offers an amazing variety of operations. The oval and figure 8 are obvious, but the trains can also be reversed without backing up, regardless of whether they are traveling around the oval clockwise or counterclockwise. You can also operate this layout as a reverse-loop to reverse-loop like the two-level plan later in this chapter.

Opposite: This layout can be operated as an oval, a figure 8, or as a loop-to-loop route.

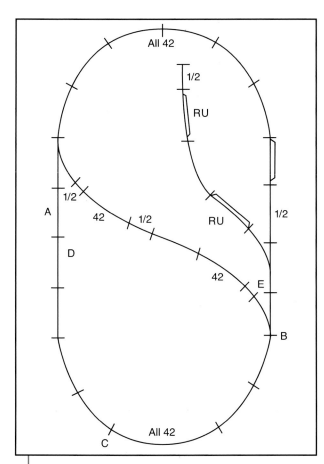

This is an oval with reverse loop cutoff and siding for 4x6 1/2 feet.

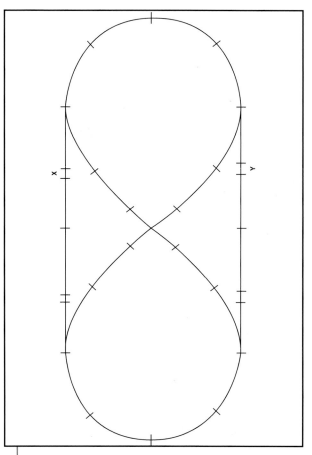

This 4x6-foot plan uses all standard 31-inch diameter curves and straights with 0-31 switches. Short filler straights may be needed at "x" and "y."

DOUBLE-TRACK MAINLINES

On a real railroad, two parallel tracks are often used on the cross-country mainline. On a model railroad, you might consider these layouts to be two ovals, one inside the other. You can use these two-oval layouts to operate two trains and allow either train to swap from running on one oval to the other. The wiring and operations are described in Chapter 7.

Only two switches (both righthand or both lefthand) are needed to create the crossover to allow trains to travel from the inner oval to the outer oval. However, the trains will have to backup to return to their original oval. By using two sets of switches, trains traveling in either direction can exit or enter the inner or outer oval.

There are two choices to assemble this layout. With O Gauge, if you use 31-inch curves for the inner oval, and 42-inch curves for the outer oval, one pair of tracks will be too close together to install a second set of crossover switches. You can also assemble the layout with two sets of O Gauge O Gauge switches by inserting a piece of half-length straight track at each end of the 42-inch oval. With FasTrack, you can use four 0-36 switches, eight 0-36 curves, and eight 0-48 curves.

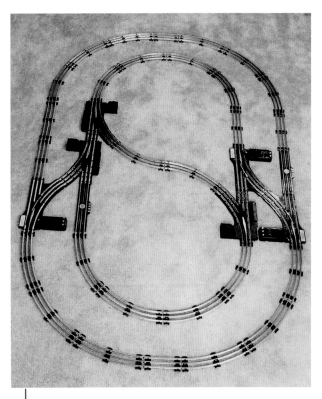

The outer oval uses 42-inch diameter curves with a single half-straight. The inner oval uses 0-31 curves, and all six switches are 0-31.

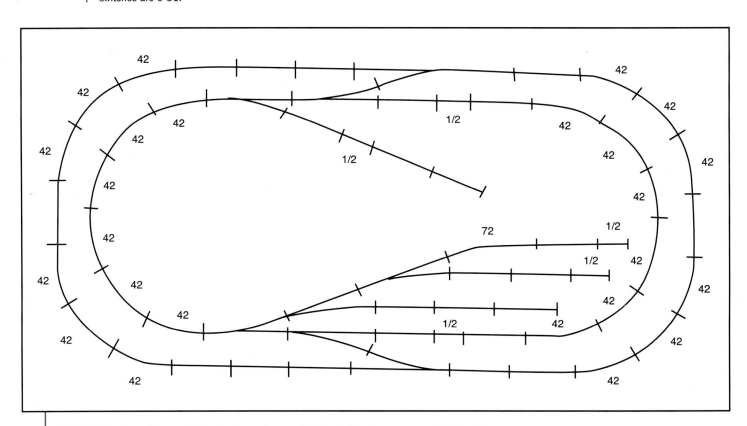

This 5x9-foot plan, with a small three-track yard, uses all 42-inch diameter curves and 0-72 switches.

PLANS FOR 0-72 SWITCHES

The 0-72 switches are the most realistic in the Lionel FasTrack line, whether your preference is 0-27, O Gauge, or FasTrack. These plans are meant to be the most versatile, considering space limitations, and they have 42-inch curves so you can operate most of the larger Lionel locomotives. The two double-track mainline layouts will fit in a 5x9-foot area, which means you could assemble them on a Ping-Pong table.

The first plan has a three-track yard so you can duplicate the train make-up and break-down switching suggested in Chapter 14. The alternate layout has a single reverse loop cutoff in place of the yard. You could squeeze a three-track yard into the reverse loop layout in place of the short siding, but the three tracks would be quite short. With either plan or a combination of the two, there's plenty of operation in just 5x9 feet.

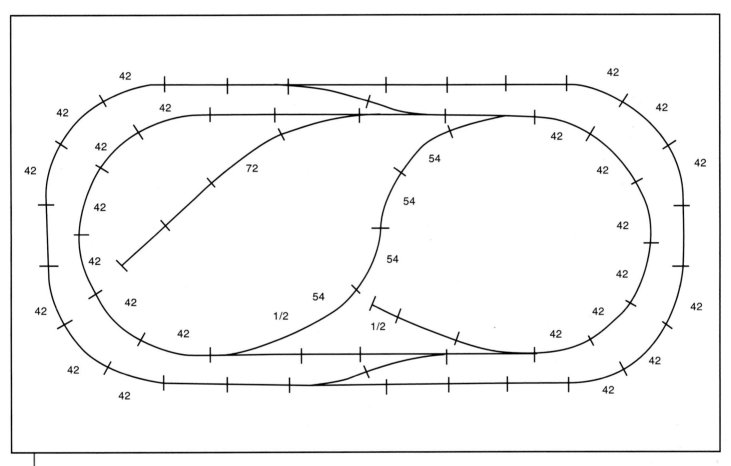

This double-track mainline with reverse loop cutoff plan will fit in a 5x9-foot area.

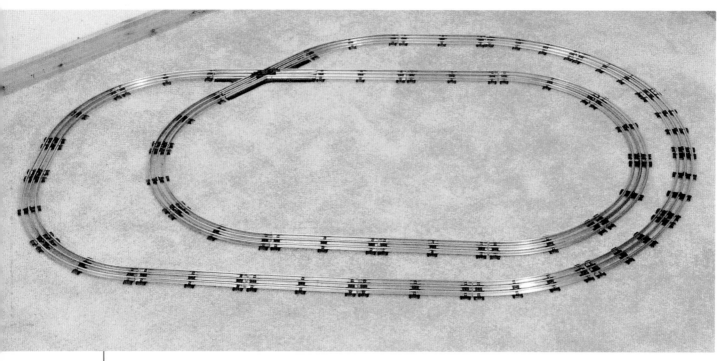

This twice-around layout is really an inverted figure 8.

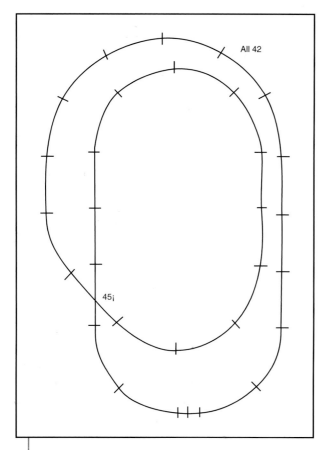

All 42

45i

This inverted figure 8 plan will fit in a 4x6-foot area.

TWO-LAP LAYOUTS

The figure 8 is one of the more interesting Lionel layouts because the tracks really do cross over themselves, and if the train is long enough, the locomotive barely clears its own caboose. This two-lap layout is a figure 8 tucked inside itself. It will fit in a 4x6-foot area.

TWO-LEVEL LAYOUTS

The exciting scene of one train passing over another is something you can re-create with Lionel track and accessories.

The Lionel Graduated Trestle Set is designed to be used with 20 sections of track (10 going up and 10 going back down). The track is elevated to 4 3/4 inches. If you want to make a larger layout, you can buy a set of elevated trestle supports to allow the elevated track to run for as far as you wish. The plastic supports clip to the metal rails and ties of O or O-27 track. Lionel has offered a number of different 26-inch-long truss bridges with either rock or concrete piers to support the ends of the bridge.

To assemble this elevated inverted figure 8, replace the 45-degree crossing with two pieces of straight track and install the elevated trestle supports, bridge piers, and bridge. The bridge piers are used to replace the two tallest elevated trestle supports.

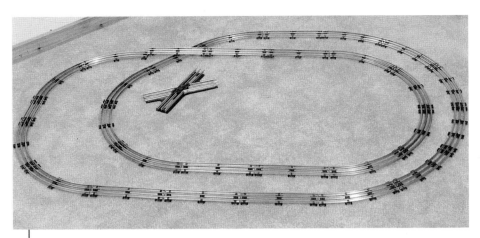

The 45-degree crossing on the inverted figure 8 layout can be replaced by two pieces of straight track and raised to make it an over and under layout.

The elevated inverted figure 8 layout requires a 4x6-foot area.

Use the Lionel graduated trestle set (6-12754) to support the track going up to and down from the bridge.

With FasTrack, the graduated trestles are designed on a 5 percent true gradient. The trestles themselves are modeled after wooden piers, or bents. The bents are spaced every 10 inches and do not need to be spaced at a track joint. There are metal stampings that run underneath the track from one bent to the next. Because of the length of the FasTrack curves, you can curve your way up the gradient even with the straight metal stampings connecting the bents underneath. In essence, there is

enough straightness to the curves to allow the connection underneath to be a straight metal stamping.

On top of the bents, there is a metal channel that the track snaps into and a pivoting head on which the track rests. This pivoting head allows for the 5 percent gradient to continue smooth and true up to the height of 5.75 inches, while still maintaining vertical bents. There are 22 sections of graduated trestles and 10 elevated trestle piers.

The two tallest graduated trestles are replaced by the piers that support the ends of the bridge.

TWO-LEVELS, LOOP-TO-LOOP

To assemble this layout, start with the lower reverse loop and the mainline that rests on the elevated trestle supports. Finish assembling the track with the upper level loop.

The graduated trestle set can be used to lift the track from the floor to the upper level. I suggest you cut a piece of 1/4-inch plywood or 1/2-inch foamcore board to support the upper loop so it can have its own "town" area.

This plan uses many 31- or 36-inch curves, so operations will be limited to smaller locomotives and shorter cars. Four short trains can be operated on this loop-to-loop layout as described in Chapter 7. The wiring for this layout is also described in Chapter 7.

The larger version of the loop-to-loop plan is 5x9 feet and can be placed on a Ping-Pong tabletop. This plan will run nearly any Lionel locomotive or car because the curves are all 42, 54, or 72 inches, and the switches are all 0-72.

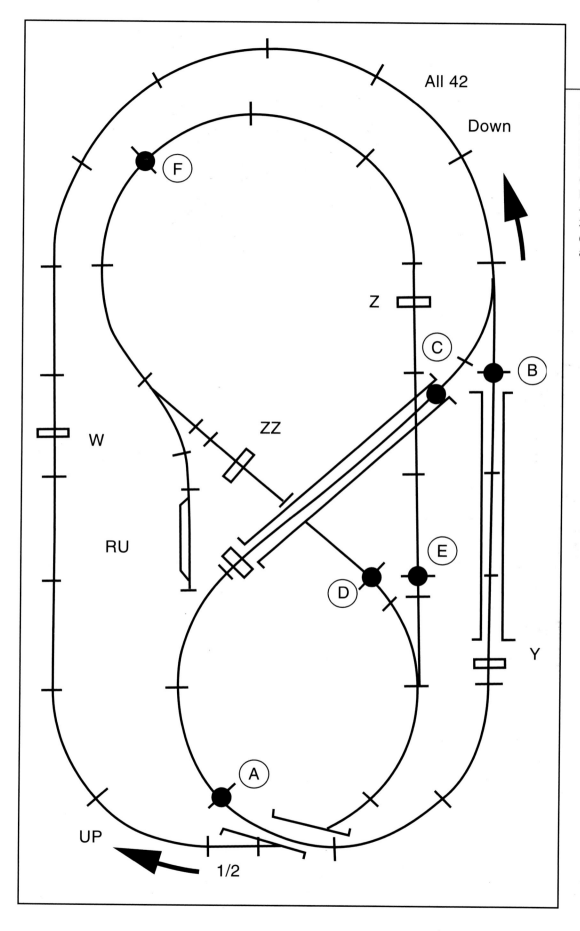

All 42

Down

One of the reverse loops on this loop-to-loop layout is elevated 4 3/4 inches above the other reverse loop. It requires just a 4x7-foot area with 31-inch diameter curves on the loops and 0-31 switches.

F

Z

C

B

ZZ

W

RU

E

D

Y

A

UP

1/2

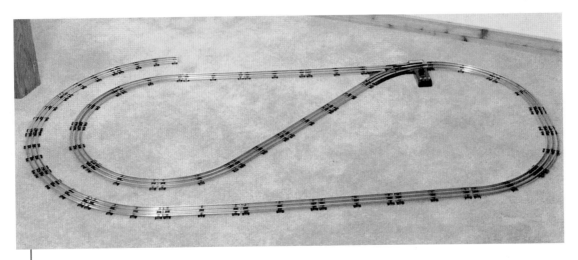

To assemble the two-level, loop-to-loop layout, begin with the lower-level loop and mainline.

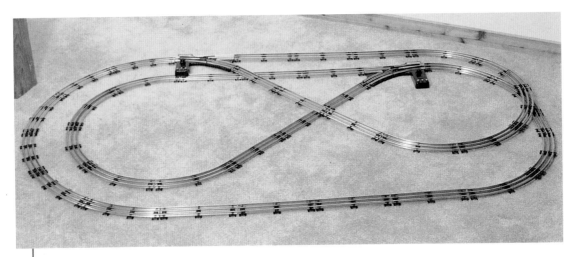

Finish the loop-to-loop layout with the upper-level loop and switch.

Use a saber saw to cut a support for the upper-level loop from 1/4-inch plywood or 1/2-inch foamcore. (Adults only, please).

The board that supports the upper-level loop rests on sturdy bricks. The Lionel graduated trestle set supports the uphill track with four of the tallest supports beneath the two truss bridges.

This is a slightly larger version of the two-level loop-to-loop layout for a 5x9-foot area, using 42-, 54-, and 72-inch diameter curves and 0-72 switches to allow large locomotives and longer trains.

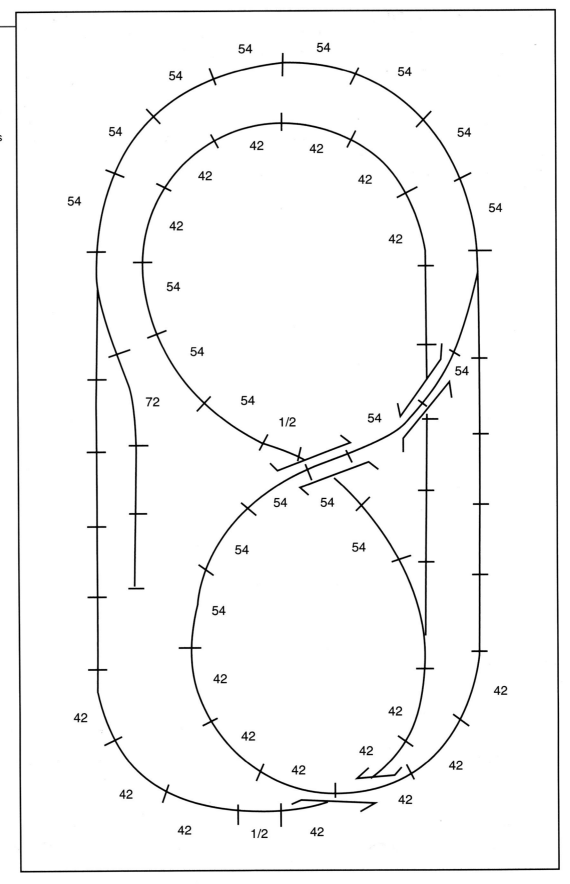

AN AROUND-THE-WALL LAYOUT

This double-track mainline is mainly a major expansion of the double-track oval for a 5x9-foot area. The plan will fill a 9 1/2x13 1/2-foot area, but it can be reduced to as small as 8x12 feet by removing three sections of track from all four double-track straightaways. The single reverse loop can be used from either of the double tracks. On a layout this large, each of the mainline tracks can be divided into four blocks so two trains can operate on both the northbound and southbound mainlines. If you are using Lionel TrainMaster Command Control, the blocks are optional because each of the four trains will be under independent control of the handheld CAB-1 Remote Controller.

RUNNING TRACK AROUND A ROOM

When you can use an entire room for your railroad, you only need a track plan for some of the restricted areas like reverse loops or the loops on one end of a figure 8. You can generally progress around the room, one track section at a time. It's a fascinating process because it's very much like building a real railroad.

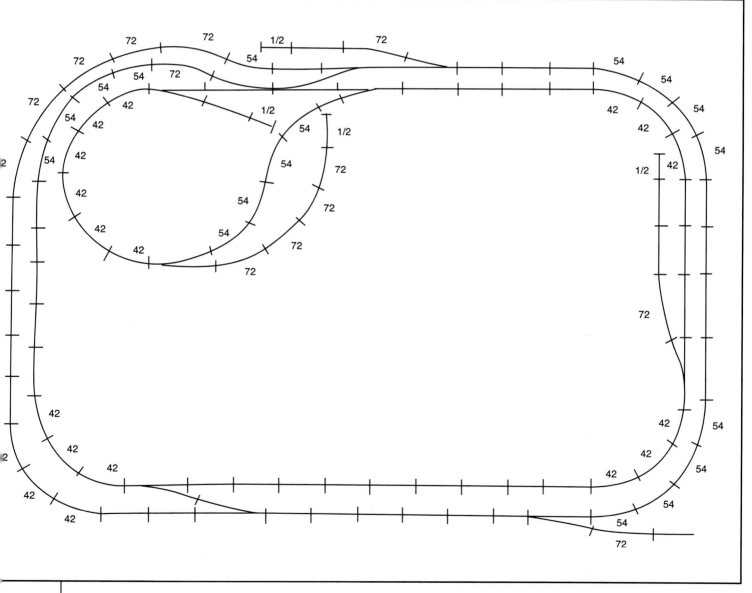

The 4x6 1/2-foot double-track plan with reverse loop cutoff expanded into an around-the-wall layout for a 9 1/2x13 1/2-foot area.

However, there's not much chance a standard track section will be the missing puzzle piece, but you can always arrange a group of two or three track sections that will fit.

In the photograph, the gap between the ends of the two 72-inch curves is too short and the angle too acute to fit any standard track section. If you remove just one of the 72-inch curves and substitute a piece of 42-inch curve joined to a piece of 54-inch curve, the gap can be filled. This combination is certainly not a rule, but an example of a nearly infinite combination of curves and half-straights that you can use to finish an around-the-floor layout.

I've used similar gap-filler track sections on several of the plans in this book, particularly when trying to join the loop of a figure 8 to a 90- or 45-degree crossing.

With FasTrack, the sheer number of half, quarter, and shorter track sections make your job of fitting your layout into your space much easier. Very few configurations are outside the capabilities of Lionel FasTrack.

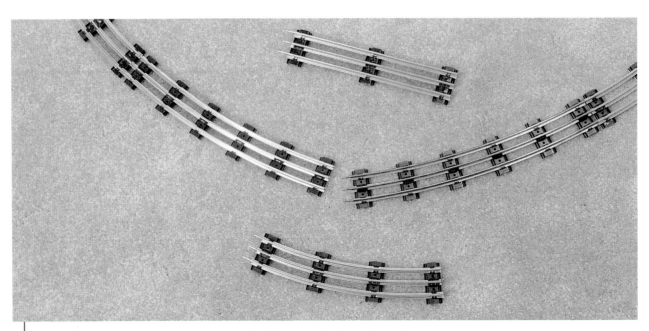

These two 72-inch diameter curves at the ends of a living-room-size layout did not line up.

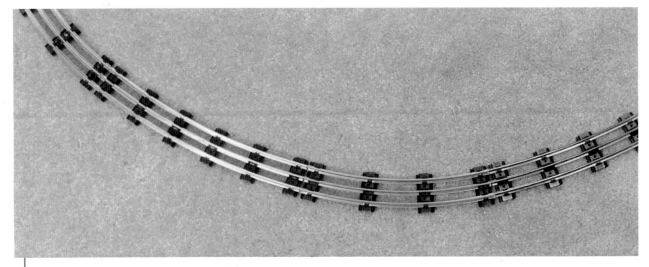

By removing one of the 72-inch diameter curves and substituting a 42-inch diameter and 54-inch diameter curve, the ends of the living-room-size layout could be accurately joined.

Chapter 4

TRACK PLANS
FOR TABLETOP LAYOUTS

The dream of most Lionel enthusiasts is to have a dedicated train table for their layout. A Lionel layout on the floor is great, but a tabletop layout becomes a miniature world.

MODEL RAILROAD BENCHWORK

Model railroaders refer to the tables as benchwork, but it's really a three-foot-high patio deck assembled indoors. Your first impulse might be to fill as much of the available space as you dare.

Before you erect that indoor patio deck, consider the possibility that you might someday want to move it to another home. One of the lessons that model railroaders have learned is to build the benchwork in framed sections that are small and light enough to be easily transported.

Most Lionel enthusiasts prefer a large tabletop that is either rectangular or L-shaped and fills half of their basements or rec rooms. You can only reach about 3 feet from the edge of a layout, so if your layout is any wider

The two Lionel's 313 Bascule Bridges on Richard Kughn's layout are placed side by side to span a small harbor inlet.

The center access aisle into Larry LaJambe's layout is disguised as a deep canyon that extends from tabletop to floor.

The benchwork on John Swanson's layout is assembled from 1"x4"s screwed together with plywood supports only beneath the tracks and structures.

than 6 feet, it will have to be built strong enough to walk on. One alternative is to place 3-foot-square access holes within the tabletop to provide a 3-foot reach area around each access hole. If you are building one of the 9x12-foot island-style layouts discussed in this chapter, you could get by with a single access hole in the middle. However, if you look at the plans carefully, you'll see there is always a track across the middle. The solution would be to cut two 3-foot-square access holes about 3 feet apart. You'll only need the access holes in an emergency, which is fortunate because they are not easy to reach.

You can also expand one of the island plans shown in this book to provide room for an open space in the center of the layout—consider it a massive "access hole" layout. The last plan in this chapter is an example of an island layout that has been expanded to fit against the walls of the room. Larry LaJambe's layout in Chapter 10 has a large access aisle that is disguised to look like a canyon.

BUILDING THE BENCHWORK

The materials you use for your model railroad benchwork will depend on how large each section of the benchwork may be (assuming you want to be able to move it out the door one piece at a time) and whether you need to build the benchwork strong enough to support your weight. If it needs to be strong enough to walk on, you'll need to use 1x4 lumber with cross braces about every 2 feet and 2x4 legs. I suggest using # 8 wood screws or even drywall screws rather than nails to assemble the benchwork.

Model railroaders, usually construct their benchwork in sections that are between 2x8 and 3x10 feet, with each section fastened with carriage bolts. It may take dozens of these sections, as with John Swanson's layout, to fill a basement, but the layout can be disassembled and moved. Most Lionel dealers can supply books about benchwork construction.

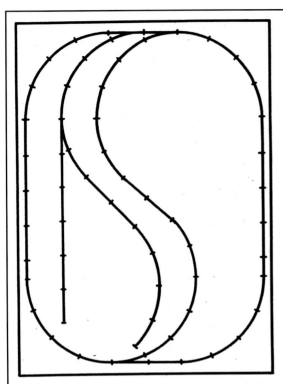

This is a variation on the oval layout. Junction of two spur tracks gives an opportunity to the model builder for using some realistic structures.

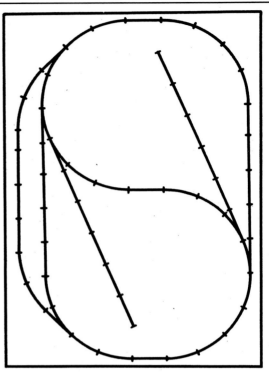

Plenty of action is packed in the passing tracks and reversing loops of this model railroad. An excellent layout for freight and passenger trains.

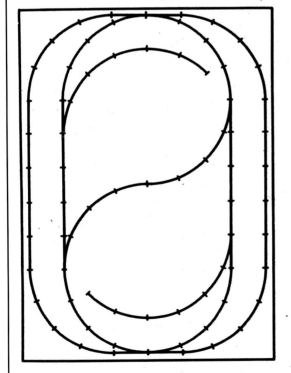

Double track oval with S-shaped connecting line and twin curved sidings. A symmetrical track arrangement for those who like a well balanced railroad.

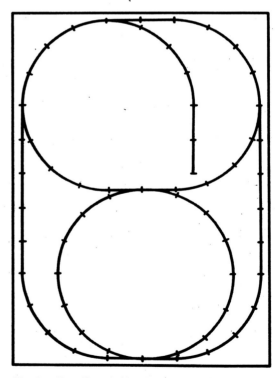

This plan will provide a railroad for the boy who wants to run his trains on a simple timetable. Double reversing loops add variety to the layout.

You can operate the largest Lionel steam locomotives on the 72-inch diameter curves and 0-72 switches shown in these four plans for 9x12-foot tabletop. *The Model Builder's Handbook, courtesy Lionel LLC*

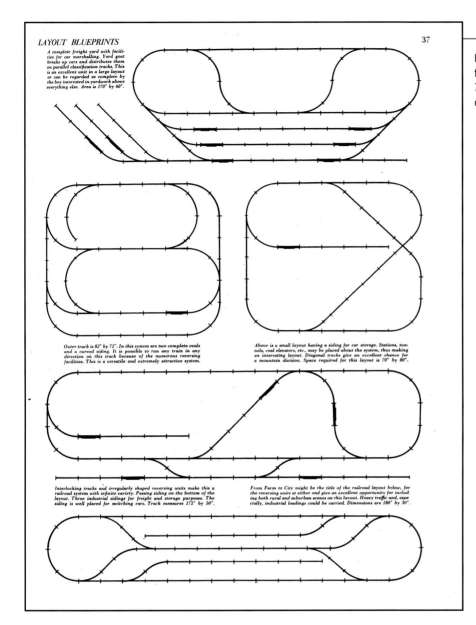

With Lionel, and the many accessories they bring to the market each year, you may want to rearrange the track, so you'll want a solid tabletop. You can use 1/4-inch plywood, but it has a resonating effect that can make operations too noisy—1/2-inch plywood is much better. You can use 1/2-inch particle board or MDF board, but the 1x4 braces will need to be placed about 18 inches apart or the board will sag. You can quiet the noise by covering the tabletop with a layer of 1-inch-thick Dow Corning Styrofoam or cover the tabletop with a 1/8-inch sheet of corkboard.

PORTABLE TABLES

That tabletop doesn't necessarily need to become a permanent part of the house. Just as Lionel track is portable, the table can also be portable.

There are many plans in this book for Lionel layouts that will fit on a 5x9-foot Ping-Pong table, including the two-level loop-to-loop layout with broad curves and 0-72 switches.

If you have the space, use two or three Ping-Pong tables. The four plans for 72-inch curves and 0-72 switches are for 9x12-foot tables. Three Ping-Pong tables, side-by-side, would measure 9x15 feet. Use C-clamps to join the edges of adjoining tables for a really sturdy structure. If you buy folding Ping-Pong tables, each table will store in just 2x5 feet of space (provided the train equipment has been removed), so a massive 9x15-foot table can be stored in 5x6 feet of floor space with room inside the folded tables for boxes of Lionel track, structures, and portable scenery.

Portable conference tables are also available in 2x8- and 2x10-foot sizes, which can be clamped together to make anything from 4x8 to 10x12 feet and more. These tables stack on their sides in about a 6-inch space, so the six tables needed for the 10x12-foot surface would store in just 3x10 feet of floor space.

A third alternative is to assemble a lightweight tabletop from 1/4-inch plywood and 2-inch blue Dow Corning Styrofoam extruded polystyrene insulation board as described in Chapter 9.

WALK-AROUND LAYOUTS

Many model railroaders build shelf-style layouts around the walls of the room. This allows them to keep the shelves to a maximum 3-foot width. The primary reason for the around-the-wall layout is so you can walk along beside your train as though you were pacing a real railroad in your car on a parallel highway . These shelf-style layouts are often built 4 to 4 1/2 feet high to place the trains nearer to eye level.

WHAT PLANS?

If you build a permanent table, you can create your own layouts. Lionel track is easy enough to assemble and disassemble so you can use the track itself to create the plan. You will not find plans in this book for the Richard Kughn, Larry LaJambe, Michael Ulewicz, or Robert Babas layouts because none exist. These large Lionel layouts, like most others, were created right on the tabletop without a plan of any sort.

PLANS FOR 9X12-FOOT TABLES

These four plans use only 72-inch curves and 0-72 turnouts so you can operate even the largest Lionel locomotives. These island-style plans are intended to be placed in the center of a room so you can walk around all four sides. There are many other island-style layout plans for spaces from 4x6 1/2 to 5x9 feet in Chapters 2 and 3.

All of these layouts include at least one reverse loop cutoff across the center of the plan. The plan that appears to be two connected ovals can actually be operated as two overlapping reverse loops.

FIVE TABLETOP TRACK PLANS

These five layouts provide a variety of concepts to help create your own Lionel layout. Remember, any plans can be enlarged by adding pairs of straight track sections on opposite sides of the layout.

The first plan is perfect for those who want to recreate the switching moves of a real railroad. The three tracks in the lower left could be a passenger terminal or freight car storage tracks. Three of the four passing sidings can be used to allow a switching locomotive to make and break down trains, one car at a time, as described in Chapter 14. This layout is 5x14 feet, but it could be built in as little as 5x9 1/2 feet if you leave out the three-track yard to the left and remove two straights from the five parallel tracks.

The two square-shaped layouts are 7x8 feet. The one on the right could be reduced to 7x5 1/2 feet if four pairs of straights were removed.

The fourth plan has reverse loop cutoff tracks for trains operating in either direction. The two stub-ended sidings at the bottom of the plan could be considered two separate towns so trains would originate at the lower left track and travel around the layout as often as you wished, using whatever routes through reverse loops seemed interesting, to arrive at the destination in the lower right.

The plan at the bottom of the page is a true loop-to-loop layout with an oval around the circumference. Again, trains could originate on one of the stub-ended siding as its city of origin to travel around the layout and through either or both reverse loops to arrive at the other stub-ended siding, its destination.

BASEMENT-SIZE PLANS

These three plans are designed to use only 72-inch curves and 0-72 switches, and they are large enough for long trains that seem to tax the largest Lionel locomotives. The L-shaped layout would fill a 10 1/2x29-foot basement. The yards tracks along the right could be reduced in length to 24 feet without doing any major harm to the operating potential of the layout.

The center layout would require 13x23 feet of tabletop, but you need to be able to walk around all four sides of the island, so it really would need a 19x29-foot room. Actually, this layout is a good candidate to operate on the floor, but if you build it on a table, it will have to be strong enough to walk on so you can reach derailed trains that are over 3 feet from the edges of the table. There are hundreds of different layout configurations you can build on a 13x23-foot table.

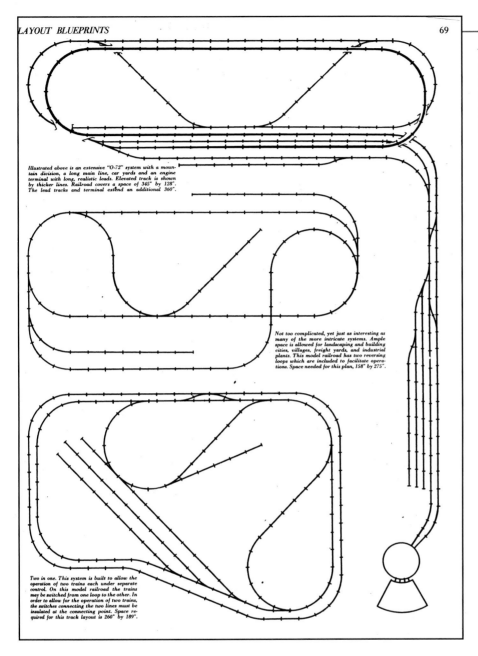

Illustrated above is an extensive "O-72" system with a mountain division, a long main line, car yards and an engine terminal with long, realistic leads. Elevated track is shown by thicker lines. Railroad covers a space of 345" by 128". The lead tracks and terminal extend an additional 360".

Not too complicated, yet just as interesting as many of the more intricate systems. Ample space is allowed for landscaping and building cities, villages, freight yards, and industrial plants. This model railroad has two reversing loops which are included to facilitate operations. Space needed for this plan, 158" by 275".

Two in one. This system is built to allow the operation of two trains each under separate control. On this model railroad the trains may be switched from one loop to the other. In order to allow for the operation of two trains, the switches connecting the two lines must be insulated at the connecting point. Space required for this track layout is 260" by 189".

These three layouts all use 72-inch diameter curves and 0-72 switches, and all are designed to fill half a basement or recreation room. *The Model Builder's Handbook, courtesy Lionel LLC*

The layout on the bottom of the page is a 22x16-foot double-track mainline with a three-track yard and reverse loops that can be used by trains traveling in either direction. This layout, like the L-shaped one, is designed for those who want to simulate real railroad operations of trains on a mainline, with a yard to make up and break down the trains and a realistic double-track mainline. This layout is a good candidate for an around-the-wall plan. Four sets of straights can be added to the four horizontal tracks at the left to move the reversing loops apart as far as you wish to make a large center access area.

AROUND-THE-WALL LAYOUTS

This delightful around-the-wall layout occupies 12x17 feet of space. If you remove nine straight track sections from each of the five parallel straight routes, you could compress the layout into an island plan to fit on a 12x9-foot table. The layout uses all 31-inch curves so, if you have more space, consider using FasTrack 36-inch curves and switches, or all 72-inch curves and 0-72 switches. With 72-inch curves, the layout should fit in about a 20x20-foot area, roughly the size of a two-car garage.

The only disadvantage to the around-the-wall layout is that you must crawl under a narrow shelf at the

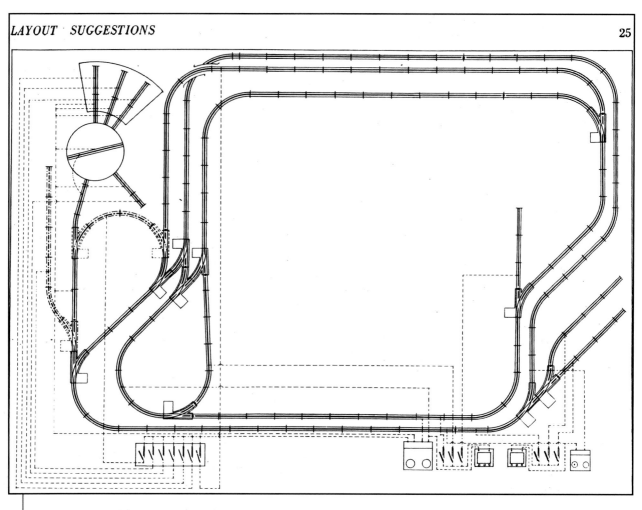

This around-the-wall layout would fill a 12x17-foot room. The Model Builder's Handbook, *courtesy Lionel LLC*

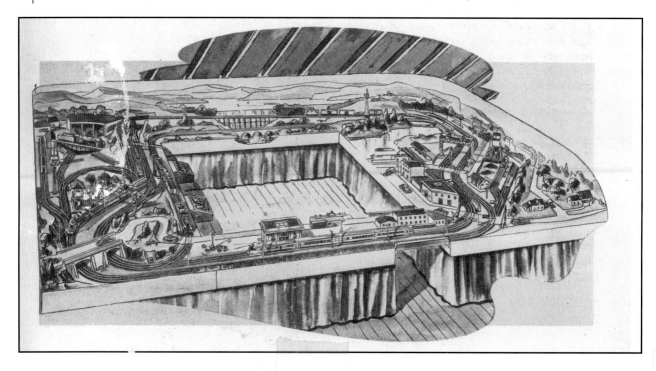

entrance to the layout. Some modelers make a 3-foot-wide removable portion of the layout. The duck-under for this layout is beneath the observation car of the passenger train. You could also use two Lionel 313 Bascule bridges, placed tip to tip, to carry a single track across a 24-inch access aisle.

THE LIONEL VISITORS CENTER LAYOUT

The massive 12x30-foot layout at the Lionel Visitors Center is an example of an island-style layout. Most of the tracks have been placed within three feet of the edge of the table so derailed trains can be reached without walking on the layout. The layout uses 150 72-inch curves, 16 0-72 switches, and 140 pieces of 40-inch (O Gauge) straight track. The upper level logging line is assembled from O-27 curves and straights. There's a second upper-level loop assembled from American Flyer track. There are many photos of the Visitor's Center layout in this book, including one of the control panel area in Chapter 6.

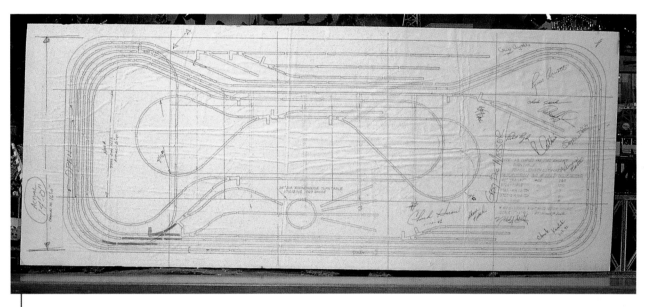

The track plan for the 12x30-foot Lionel Visitors Center layout was signed by the dozen people who built the real one in 1992.

This is the southeast, or "mountain" end, of the Lionel Visitors Center layout, and the control panel is on the far left.

Here's the northwest corner of the Lionel Visitors Center layout.

The southwest corner of the Lionel Visitors Center layout is pictured, and the logging railroad is visible in the upper center.

The exact-scale Pennsylvania Railroad S-2 steam turbine fills the 36-inch turntable on the Lionel Visitors Center layout.

An American Flyer GP-7 in Wabash colors pulls a freight on the upper loop of the Lionel Visitors Center layout, while a logging and coal train is exiting the tunnel on the middle level.

A Heisler pulls a log train on the middle-level loop of the Lionel Visitors Center layout. The upper-level track is American Flyer.

Chapter 5

TRACK

Lionel O and O-27 trains were designed to run on three-rail track. The outer two rails are spaced so the wheel flanges on the locomotive and cars will grip the inside edges of the rails to keep the trains on the track. The center rail provides electrical pickup. It is on constant contact with the rollers on the bottom of all the locomotives and on any freight or passenger cars that have inside lighting or other electrical devices. The third rail makes it much easier to assemble and wire the electrical connections on a Lionel layout as described in Chapter 6.

LIONEL TRACK

Currently, Lionel offers three major types of track: O-27, O, and FasTrack. Any Lionel train will operate on any of these tracks. The only exceptions are Lionel Large Scale,

Michael Ulewicz added wood ties and ballast to his track. The ties and ballast are cemented firmly together with artist's matte medium and water.

Lionel 0-72 switches and 72-inch diameter curves were used on this corner of Richard Kughn's layout with loose ballast glued firmly in place.

Lionel's FasTrack (left) is far more realistic than the classic 0-31 track.

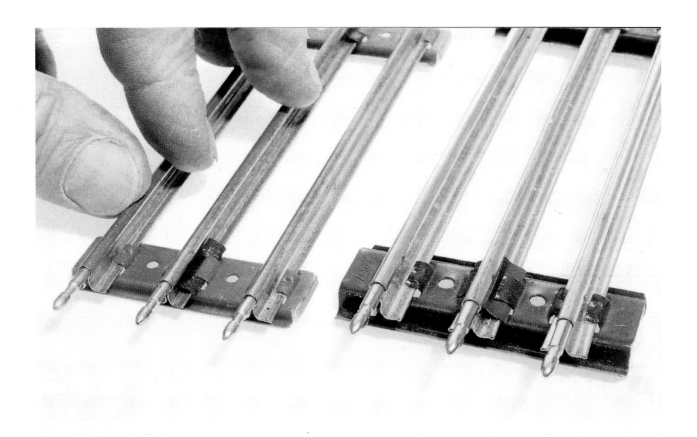

The rails and ties are smaller on O-27 track (left) than on O Gauge track, but Lionel trains will run on either size track.

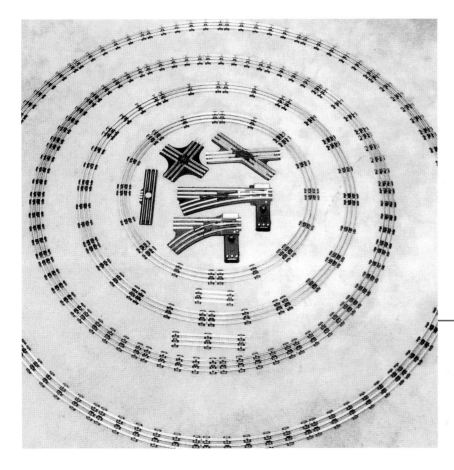

There is a wide range of track available in the O Gauge size including 31-, 42-, 54-, and 72-inch diameter curves, half-length straights, full-length straights, 40-inch straights (not shown), remote-control track, 45-degree crossing, 90-degree crossing, and 31- and 72-inch path switches.

American Flyer, and Lionel HO. Lionel lists the minimum operating track curve diameters both in the catalogs and on the product packaging.

The O-27 track is the lightest, lowest profile, and tightest diameter of all Lionel track. The straight track sections are 8 3/4-inches long, and a 35-inch straight is available. There are also O-27-, 42-, and 54-inch diameter curved track sections offered. Half-length straights and half-length O-27 curves are available, as well as 45- and 90-degree crossover sections. Some modelers prefer the lighter weight and prototypical profile (height at the top of the rails) of O-27 track and switches. Be aware that you may not be able to operate the very largest Lionel locomotives on O-27 track because 72-inch curves are not available in O-27.

The oldest Lionel track offered today is O Gauge, often referred to as "0 Gauge." The standard lengthO Gauge straight tracks for O Gauge are 10 inches long, and a 40-inch-long straight is available. The O Gauge track is available in 31-, 42-, 54-, and 72-inch diameter curves. There is also a half-length straight, a half-length O Gauge curve, and a 45- and a 90-degree crossover sections. O Gauge is more rugged and has a higher profile than O-27. It is meant to be ballasted when mounted on a permanent layout, similar to how real track rails are across America.

LIONEL FASTRACK

The most realistic looking, and rapidly becoming the most popular, Lionel track is FasTrack with its simulated ballast and more realistic ties. The standard length straight for FasTrack is 10 inches (6-12014), and there is a 30-inch straight (6-12042) and a 10-inch Terminal Track (6-12016).

FasTrack is available in 036 curves (6-12015) that require the same eight pieces to make a circle as O-27 or O Gauge standard curves. There is also a 1/2 0-36 and a 1/4 0-36 curve. FasTrack also includes 48-, 60-, and 72-inch curves. It takes 12 sections of 0-48 to make a circle, and 16 each of 0-60 and 0-72 to make a circle. The 0-72 half curve track joins the line as an added layout tool. There is a 90-degree FasTrack crossover 22.5 degree and 44 degree crossover sections.

The FasTrack line includes 1 3/4-, 4 1/2-, and 5-inch (or half) straights. If you need a length of track not covered by these three options, you can combine the

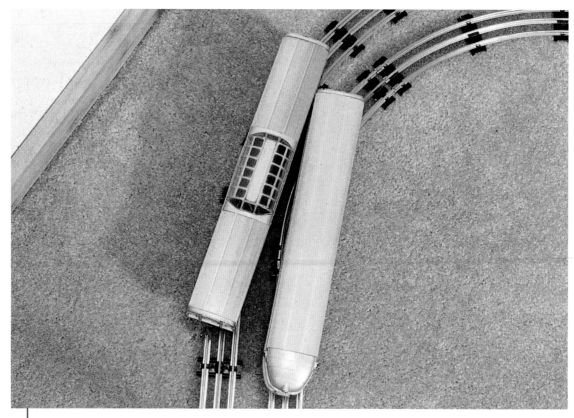

The longer passenger cars and freight cars can sideswipe each other, especially if the overhanging ends contact the underhanging middle. You can usually shift the track a few inches to avoid the problem.

three to make up the difference. If you need 1 inch of straight track, you can use a 10-inch straight track in the spot where you need the extra inch and place two 4 1/2-inch straights on the opposite side of the layout. There are many combinations that can be used to obtain the exact length of filler track you might need on a complex layout. The trick is to be patient and use your math skills. To stay up to date on FasTrack, consult the latest Lionel catalog, the Lionel website (www.lionel.com), or see your local dealer.

INTERCHANGING O-27, O GAUGE, AND FASTRACK

We recommend using all of one type of track for your layout, but if you are switching between Lionel track systems, you can connect O-27 track to O Gauge track by opening the O-27 rails with an awl to accept the larger O Gauge track pins and squeezing the O Gauge rails with pliers so they will clamp the smaller O-27 track pins more tightly, but this is not recommended. If you choose to use O-27 and O Gauge track on the same layout, they should be confined to totally separate loops. Since FasTrack has the same profile as O Gauge, you can easily build a layout using both track types on the same loop. Use the FasTrack O Gauge Transition Piece to adapt O Gauge track to FasTrack.

MINIMUM-SIZE CURVES

The curves on any model railroad are much tighter than those on any real railroad. The trains are designed to negotiate these tight curves, but there are physical limitations. Most of the larger Lionel steam locomotives require wide diameter curves to avoid derailment. To know whether a particular piece of equipment will work on your existing or planned layout, refer to the Lionel catalogs and packaging to determine minimum turn diameters. They are labeled clearly to avoid unpleasant surprises or railway mishaps. Since switches have a curved route or path, you should consider using the 72-inch path remote control switches for larger locomotives. There are several track plans in Chapters 3 and 4 for layouts that have 0-72 switches, even using curved track sections as tight as 42 or 54 inches. Lionel also includes plans for layouts with no turns sharper than a 72-inch-diameter curve with matching switches. Frankly, the 72-inch switches are by far the most realistic, since the long engines tend not to overhang the track when entering or exiting curves.

Practically speaking, the longer locomotives and extended freight and passenger cars can also derail on closely situated double-track loops where the overhanging parts of one car might sideswipe a car on an adjacent track. Lionel has selected curve sizes to minimize the chance of sideswiping on curves. If you use the O-27 size 27-, 42-, or 54-inch curves; the O Gauge size 31-, 42-, 54-, and 72-inch curves; or the FasTrack 36-, 48-, 60-, and 72-inch curves, the trains will not derail one another. You must, however, keep the spacing even from one track to another all the way around the entire layout. On some plans, the spacing between parallel straight sections can safely be closer than that on the curves. Before you operate two trains at once, take the two longest cars and manually run them through curves, side-by-side, and adjust the spacing to see if you see the possibility of one car hitting the center of the other.

LIONEL SWITCHES

Lionel offers O-27, O, and FasTrack switches in various diameters, routes, or pads. Three switches are available for O-27: the 27-inch path manual switch, the 27-inch path remote-control switches, and the 42-inch path remote-control switches.

There are two O Gauge switches available; the 31-inch path remote-control switches and the 72-inch path remote-control switches.

The FasTrack line includes switches with 33.75 degree curved-route manual switches or remote switches. FasTrack remote switches with 72-inch-diameter curved routes (22.5 degree) are also available. For more complex layouts, FasTrack also features the O-72 remote switch, which is especially helpful in configuring train hump yards. Other expert modeler FasTrack switches will join the Lionel line as time goes on.

Using modern electronics, FasTrack switches require less power than any other O Gauge switch and are equipped with terminals to easily connect them to the TrainMaster Command Control SC-2 or ASC switch control units for totally remote operation anywhere on the layout using a CAB-1 Remote Controller.

UNCOUPLING AND REMOTE-CONTROL TRACKS

Uncoupling and remote-control tracks are used to provide hands-off train-building operations and to activate action cars that dump logs or coal or unload milk cans, mail bags, crates, and barrels. Most of these devices are actuated by an electromagnet placed between the rails that attracts a coin-size steel disc below the couplers or near the center of the car (to trigger action cars). The electromagnet between the rails receives its power from the third rail and is activated by a push button that you can place near your transformer.

Some of the larger Lionel cars and locomotives and some equipment from the Postwar era are fitted with couplers that can only be actuated (for uncoupling) electrically through small rectangular pickup shoes on the bottoms of the trucks. These pickup shoes are designed to contact a fourth and fifth rail in the Lionel remote-control track. Remote-control tracks also have an electromagnet in the center to actuate couplers and activate action cars.

The O-27 and O Gauge remote-control tracks have a controller with two push buttons, and there are four wires to connect to the screw posts on the track. The O-27 uncoupling track has a single push button and two wires to connect it to the track section.

The FasTrack uncoupling track will operate Lionel couplers or action cars equipped with steel discs on the bottom. The FasTrack remote control track is designed to activate couplers or action cars that have the pickup shoes for the fourth and fifth rails. It accomplishes the task of remote coupler/action activation without appearing to be special or different from regular FasTrack sections.

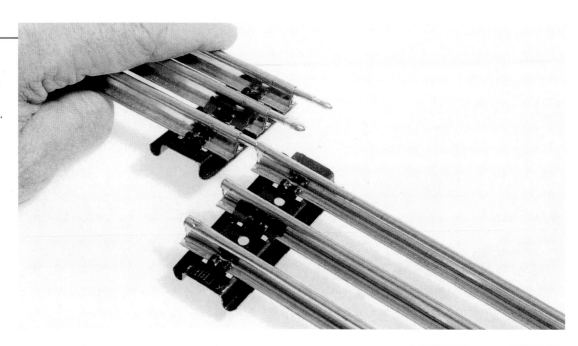

You can use a second piece of track to pry open tight rail ends.

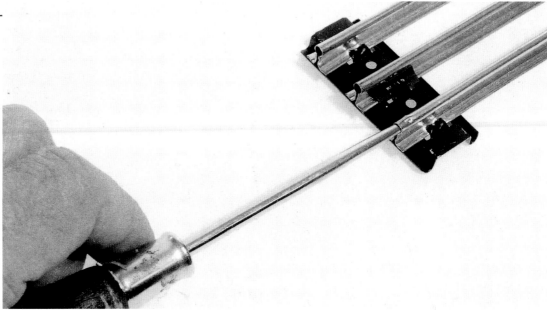

If the rail end is bent, it can be straightened with the tip of an awl or an ice pick.

LIONEL LARGE SCALE TRACK

Two-rail track for Large Scale models with 1 3/4 inches between the rails are also offered. The Large Scale track sections include a standard straight that is 11 3/4 inches long, a 51 1/2-inch-diameter curved track, a 63 1/2-inch-diameter wide-radius curved track. This track is constructed with tubular brass rails and can be used indoors or outdoors. A Lockon for Large Scale track is also available. This system operates on DC current and isn't compatible with Lionel O or O-27 track products.

AMERICAN FLYER TRACK

Lionel does not offer two-rail track for American Flyer. Lionel dealers generally maintain inventories of used American Flyer track and switches for sale, and S Gauge hobbyists regularly offer it for trade or sale at local and national model train swap meets.

ASSEMBLING O AND O-27 LIONEL TRACK

Lionel track, with its steel rails and track pins, is extremely rugged, and cam be assembled and disassembled many times, but there is a minimum requirement of

Squeeze the ends of both rails and angle the pliers toward the inside of the track.

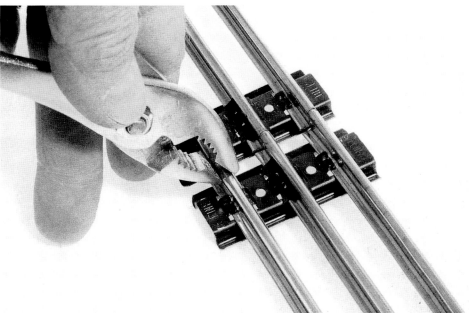

Squeeze the track again to tighten the rail ends, with the pliers rotated about 90 degrees toward the outside of the track.

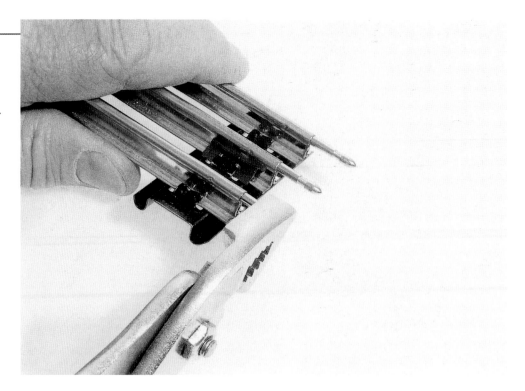

To remove a metal track pin, hold the track pin as shown and gently lever against the base of the rail and pull it straight out.

care and maintenance during its lifespan. Some track users will assemble a track layout, play with it for a while, and disassemble it and store it in boxes until the next time it is needed. If some care isn't taken in its storage, you might find some of the rail ends may be bent so that no amount of effort will get that track section to connect to any others. This can often be fixed by prying open the too-tight rail end by using the end rail of a second piece of track to work the rail end open. If the end of the rail has been bent too tightly, carefully use an awl (adults only, please) to pry the open end of the rail apart until a track pin can push in with the same amount of effort you would normally need for other track joints.

A more common condition, the open ends of the track rails will be pried open a little too wide and won't make a snug connection with the track pins. This can

Use a hack saw to cut special-length track sections, but hold the rails—not the ties—firmly in a vise while you saw.

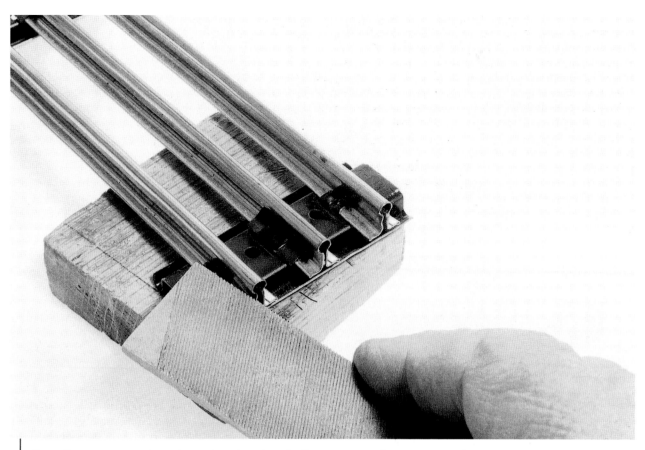

Use a file to remove any sharp edges or burrs from the rails. Clean the inside of the rail with a knife.

happen if you accidentally kick the track when it is on floor or if you try to pick up a line of several assembled sections of track without proper support and they bend in the air. It can also occur with repeated regular use. To tighten a loose rail end, assemble it to the next section of track. Use needlenose pliers to crimp down the loose rail ends from one side of the rail, then rotate the pliers about 90 degrees over the top of the rails and crimp the other side. Try not to apply excessive pressure because it will cause the plier jaws to dig into the track rail surface, which promotes rust—the enemy of good electrical contact. You will be able to feel how much pressure is right. Just keep in mind you want to have a snug fit, not a tight fit, and all will be fine.

When you use O and O-27 track, you will need to remove track pins from curved tracks so you can reinsert them on the other end of the rails and change right turn curve to left turn curves, and vice versa. To remove a steel track pin, hold the pin as close to the end of the rail as possible. Using needlenose pliers, gently pry the pin about 1/16 inch out of the rail, wiggle it slightly to loosen it, then use the pliers to pull the pin straight out

of the end of the rail. Rebend the base of the rail if it was loosened in the process.

Each section of Lionel steel track has holes in every tie (and FasTrack has holes between the ties that can be easily punched through) so you can insert round-head wood screws to attach the track to a plywood or MDF tabletop.

If you are not going to fasten the track to the tabletop, you may want install the Lionel O Gauge track clips across the bottom of the ties at each joint to keep of the tracks firmly connected. Lionel also offers an O-27 track clip, shown in Chapter 3.

Assembling FasTrack is a snap. Because it uses both pins and a snap fit on the plastic base, the electrical connection is superior and the physical connection between sections is rock solid. Further, FasTrack pins are cleverly designed so that you never have to pull them out. Every curved track can be either left or right without any adjustment. Best of all, the pins never loosen the fit with the rails, so the days of crimping rail sections are over. There is no better track for beginning railroaders, and hobbyists have begun laying FasTrack.

CUSTOM-FITTED O AND O-27 TRACK

If you are building a complex Lionel layout, you may discover that you need to cut special-length track sections for every track joint to align perfectly. The Lionel O-27 and O Gauge straight or curved track sections can be cut with a hacksaw. Clamp the rails of the track, not the ties, in a vise while sawing so you can guide the saw blade properly, and be sure the cut is perpendicular to the rails. When the cut is complete, file the edges to eliminate sharp spots or burrs. If you don't have a vise or hacksaw, your Lionel service station may be able to cut the track for you or suggest a local machine shop that can assist you. FasTrack offers a large selection of track sections in various lengths to virtually eliminate the need to cut anything.

TRACK MAINTENANCE

If you run your trains, your Lionel track will get dirty. The constant arcing of electrical current, traces of oil thrown from diesel wheels and steam drivers, metal filings from rotating wheels and axels and airborne grit will settle on the tops of the rails. Before you clean the track, vacuum all excess debris with a brush attachment and an extension hose. Next, dust the track and switches with a 1-inch-wide paint brush and wipe it clean with a lint-free rag. The Lionel lubrication/maintenance set includes gear lube, an oil applicator, track-cleaning fluid, a track-cleaning eraser, and instructions. Apply a little track-cleaning fluid to a clean rag and wipe the track-cleaning fluid over the tops of every inch of all three rails. Make sure you're in a well ventilated area. Wipe the rails clean with another rag. Gently scrub the tops of all the rails with the track-cleaning eraser and use a clean rag dampened with track-cleaning fluid to wipe away any residue from the eraser.

SWITCH MAINTENANCE

The O and O-27 remote-control switches rely on tried-and-true Lionel design. Refined slightly over the years, the basic operating mechanisms have been around for decades. The 72-inch path remote-control switches (often called O-72 switches)also have a very similar

Clean the moving switch point center rail with a track-cleaning eraser to ensure stall-free performance. Wipe the top of all the switch third rails and the tops of all the other rails with Lionel track-cleaning fluid on a clean rag.

design, but are longer with a more gradual turnout section. The O-27 switches, including the 27-inch path switches, 27-inch path remote-control switches, and 42-inch path remote-control switches have a similar swivel rail to change the path of the trains from straight to curve, but the operating mechanism is somewhat different from the O Gauge or 0-72 switches.

The 31- and 72-inch path O Gauge switches have the control box (switch machine) mounted to the side of the switch. The control box can be moved by removing two screws and shifting it to the opposite side of the track for locations where clearance might be needed on one side or the other.

Turn the switch upside down so you can reach the two Phillips-head screws located diagonally on the bottom beneath the switch point area. Remove the two screws and note that each is threaded into a flat-top, blind-end hex nut that drops in from the rail side of the switch. These nuts will likely fall out when you remove the screws, so watch for them. Gently lift the control box from the bottom of the switch.

Look closely at the control box and you will see a round brass or black plastic pin protruding upward. That pin engages a slot beneath the switch points to move the switch points from the straight to the curved route. When you reassemble the switch, that pin must engage the slot beneath the switch points.

Remove the three knurled nuts from the wire-connecting posts and remove the two black Phillips-head screws that hold the control box cover. Pull the rotating lamp cover away from the top of the control box and remove the control-box lid.

There is a small gear that drives a rack (a straight row of gear teeth), which controls the rotating lamp cover. When the switch is activated to move the route from curved to straight, the rack moves the gear to rotate the lamp cover so that the red or green lenses show down the track. You can operate these switches manually by holding the rotating lamp cover and twisting it. Check to see that the gear teeth are not chipped and clean off any residue. Apply just a trace of Lionel lube with a toothpick to the gear teeth.

Rotate the lamp cover gear to see how the sliding plate moves in the control box. There are copper or nickel silver contact strips on either side of the sliding strip in the area that lies beneath the moving switch point. Clean each of those contacts with Lionel track-cleaning fluid and polish them with the track-cleaning

Remove the two shiny Phillips-head screws from the bottom of the 0-31 or (shown) 0-72 switch to remove the switch machine from the switch base.

The switch machine can be mounted on either side of the 0-31 or 0-72 switches. The black plastic or brass vertical pin moves to actuate the switch points.

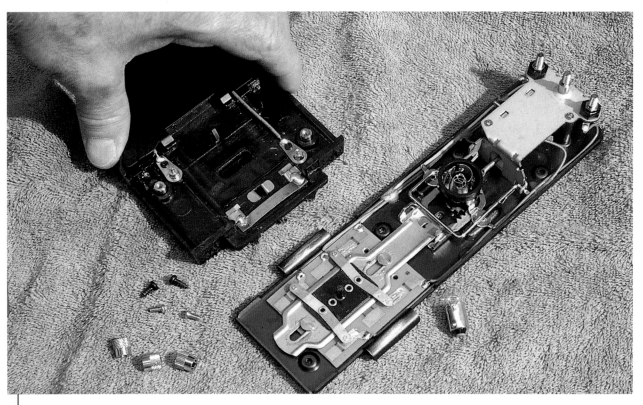

Unscrew the three knurled terminal-post nuts and the two black Phillips-head screws to remove the cover from the O-31 and O-72 switch machine.

The black gear-toothed rack engages the teeth on a spur gear to turn the lamp on the switch machine.

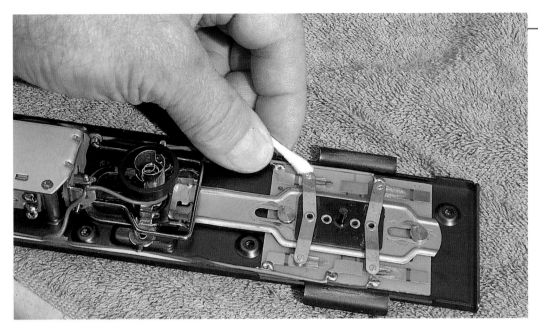

Move the switch points to the straight route and clean the two exposed contacts with a cotton swab dipped in track-cleaning fluid. Next move the sliding arm to the curved position and clean the remaining two contacts. Polish the clean contacts with a track-cleaning eraser.

eraser. Move the switch to the alternate position and clean and polish those contacts.

Use a small paint brush to sweep away any dust from inside the control box. Replace the control box lid and the two black screws that hold it in place. Thread the three terminal post nuts onto the posts and snap the rotating lamp cover in place. Connect the control box to the bottom of the switch, starting with the single brass pin that engages the mechanism. Be sure that pin is in the proper slot before pushing the control box gently in place. Test the switch by moving the switch points and rotating lamp cover before you insert the final two screws and nuts. Tighten until they are secure.

IMPROVED SWITCH PERFORMANCE

You can run your switches directly off track power, but depending on the size of your layout and number of switches, you may find that this will divert too much power from your mainline train operations. For that reason, I recommend that you use a separate power supply, commonly referred as fixed power, for your Lionel remote-control switches, just as you would when adding operating accessories. If your switches don't throw completely or move very slowly, the cause could be a lack of electrical power.

Lionel 31- and 72-inch diameter remote-control switches come with a small black plug with a screw in

This vertical pin must engage the slot below the switch points when you reassemble the switch machine to the bottom of the switch.

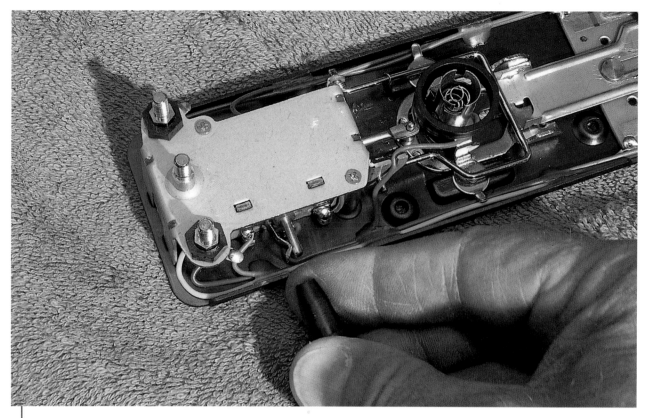

The plug for the Lionel 0-31 and 0-72 switches opens copper contacts to allow the current to operate the switch from a separate power supply.

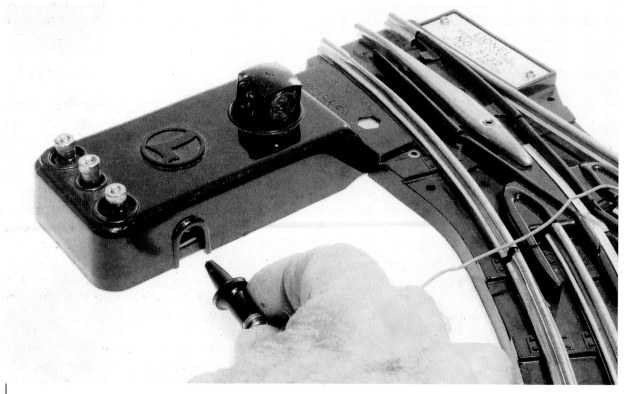

The plug to provide electrical power from a separate power supply is plugged into a slot at the bottom edge of the switch machine.

Ralph Johnson used a Lionel No. 375 remote-control turntable for the engine yard on his layout.

one end. That plug is designed to fit in a socket on the lower edge of the control box. Connect a wire from that socket to the accessory power supply and plug it into the control box. That's all that is needed to provide direct power to each Lionel switch. The ground or second wire is one of the track rails, so only one wire is needed for each switch. The special plug automatically disconnects electrical power from the rails and leaves only the electrical ground rail connection.

FasTrack remote-control switches also come equipped with separate fixed power connections.

LOCOMOTIVE TURNTABLES

Real railroads once used turntables to reverse the direction of steam locomotives, which, because of the position of the backhead and controls, offered only limited reverse operation capability. Diesels can be run with the cab facing the front or rear, and often the railroads coupled two or more diesels together with the cabs at the ends facing opposite directions so the diesels did not need to be turned around. Many real railroads still use turntables to turn diesels, since most engineers prefer to run the short end of hood diesels facing forward, and, of course, the cab end of cab diesels must go first. Turntables are also used to turn passenger cars and observation cars, and, in some cases, dining cars can be

turned so the food-receiving door would be on the side with the easiest access.

Turntables were also usually equipped with several tracks leading to the roundhouse building, where the locomotives were stored and serviced between runs. Thus the turntable could serve to index locomotives into specific roundhouse stalls and turn the locomotives end-for-end.

Lionel offered a No. 375 remote-control turntable for a few years in the early 1960s. You may be able to find a used one at your authorized Lionel dealer, or at a local model train swap meet.

In the meantime, you can use a lazy Susan to convert into a turntable. To transform a 24-inch lazy Susan into a turntable, assemble a length of straight track to extend about 1/4 inch beyond the edges of the lazy Susan. You might be able to use standard and partial-length straights, but with O and O-27 track, you may need to custom cut a track section to get the correct length. If you do, put that custom track section in the middle of the lazy Susan.

Most undecorated lazy Susans are a light shade of beige or brown. You may want to paint yours dark brown or black so it looks more realistic. Attach the track with silicone caulking compound. The lazy Susan will probably be 1/2 inch or higher than the level of the track that leads up to it, so you will need to elevate the tracks on either end of the turntable with a stack of three or more 1/4x5/8-inch strips of balsa or bass wood cut into 2 1/4-inch-long ties that have been dyed or painted black or dark brown. In operation, you will need to revolve the turntable by hand and hold it steady while the locomotive runs on and off the turntable track.

The simplest method of powering the turntable is to attach a Lockon to the nearest O or O-27 powered track or place a FasTrack terminal track at the end of the section leading to the end of the section leading up to the lazy Susan, connect two wires (long enough to allow a 180-degree, or half-rotation, of the turntable) from the Lockon or terminal track, and crimp an alligator clip onto the end of each of the wires. Connect the alligator clips to the bottom edge of the track rails on the lazy Susan, being careful to connect the outside and center rail wires to the appropriate outside and center rails—in a continuous line—to match the connections at the Lockon. When the locomotive has been driven onto the turntable, turned, and run off, disconnect the alligator clips from the track ends and clip them onto the edge of the lazy Susan, keeping them apart so they don't get tangled or touch each other and cause a short circuit, which would temporarily shut down the transformer.

In lieu of a turntable, some locomotive and car assembly shops used to employ a bridge, called a transfer table, that would shift left and right to align the track with stalls in a rectangular engine house or shop. The transfer table can index locomotives or cars onto parallel tracks, but it cannot turn a locomotive or car end-for-end. Lionel has offered several transfer tables through the years, including the No. 350 engine transfer table, along with two-track extensions for multi-track operations. This accessory should be relatively easy to locate for those who are interested.

MORE REALISTIC TRACK FOR O AND O-27 OPERATORS

Many Lionel fans prefer the shiny appearance of three-rail tinplate track. Lionel all-steel track is also extremely strong and has been proven over many decades of operation. You can improve its realism by adding additional ties to fill in the larger gaps. Cut additional ties from 1/4x5/8-inch strips of balsa or basswood. Use a razor saw (adults only, please) to cut them into

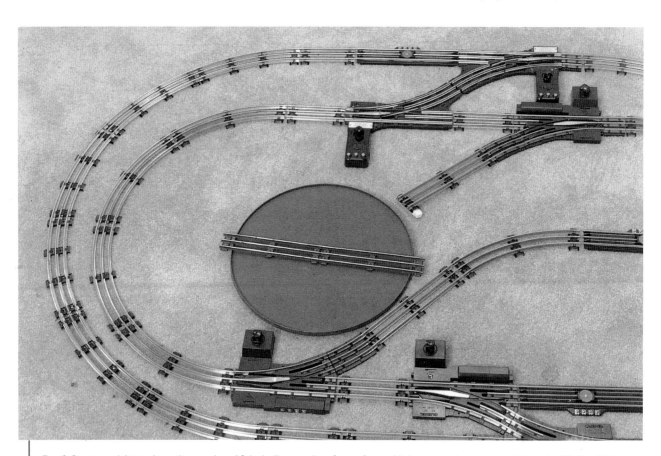

Two O Gauge straight-track sections and an 18-inch-diameter lazy Susan from a kitchenware store were used to make this turntable.

2 1/4-inch-long ties. Use dark brown dye to stain or use a realistic shade of brown to paint the ties a nice creosote shade. You can cement the ties to the rails with a sticky cement like Shoe Goo or Barges Cement, available at most craft, hobby, and train stores.

Real railroad ties are held in place with ballast. Using loose dirt or grit of any kind is risky on a model railroad, and I would not recommend using ballast for a portable model railroad. If you are building a permanent Lionel layout, you can glue the track down and cover the track up to about 1/2 inch of the ends of the ties with loose ballast. Your Lionel dealer can supply several types and brands of O scale ballast. Sprinkle the ballast in place and use a small paint brush to remove any excess from the tops of the ties. Keep the ballast away from switches and carefully cover each switch with a plastic sandwich bag and tape it to the edges so no ballast or cement can work its way into the switch mechanism. When you are satisfied with the shape of the ballast (make sure the height of the ballast is at least 1/8 inch below the top of the rails), mix equal parts water and artist's matte medium and add a few drops of dish detergent to break the water's surface tension so it

will penetrate and not ball up. Using a spray bottle, spray the ballast and the track until the area is a milky gray and let it dry for about a week. You will need to clean the matte medium off the tops of the rails with a Lionel track-cleaning eraser or similar slightly abrasive material before running your trains.

INSTANT REALISM WITH FASTRACK

Lionel FasTrack is the simple way to enjoy three-rail operation with realistic, highly detailed track. FasTrack uses well-proportioned, molded-in ties, even at the switches and crossings, and the simulated ballast forms the base of each track section. With molded ballast, there are no loose particles to jam locomotives or switches. FasTrack can be used for portable or permanent layouts. You can assemble FasTrack on the floor and rearrange it every week if you like, or you can attach it to a permanent tabletop with a bead of silicone caulking cement along the bottom edge of the ballast. If you want to move the track, just pry it up gently with a screwdriver and peel off the dried silicone. If you want to attach the track to the tabletop with screws, each track section has holes to accommodate the No. 4 3/4-inch flathead sheet-metal screws.

The ballasted track on the Lionel Visitors Center layout is not as realistic as the smaller ties and molded-in ballast on Lionel FasTrack.

Troubleshooting Track

Symptom: Train derails

1. Check each track joint to be sure it is firmly in place. Wiggle the track slightly to make sure the rail ends have not been enlarged so much that the track pins are loose. If any joints are loose, use the techniques in this chapter to tighten them with pliers. Lay your head on the track and look down the rails to spot any severe dips or humps at track joints that can cause derailments.

2. If the derailment occurs only at one track section, check that piece to be sure one of the rails has not bent or worked its way free of the metal clamps on the ties. If the section is doubtful, replace it with a new one to see if that cures the derailment problem.

3. If the derailment occurs at a switch, be sure the switch is thrown in the correct position. Check for debris along the inside of all the outer rails. Make sure that the moving parts of the switch and the switch points have solid contact with the proper outside rail.

4. Sometimes derailments are caused by problems with locomotives or cars. Look carefully to see if there is just one set of wheels on the locomotive or car that derails. Some larger Lionel locomotives and longer cars can derail on O 27 or 0-31 switches or curves. Some larger locomotives require 54-inch-diameter curves as a minimum, and some require 72-inch curves.

Symptom: Switch does not throw

1. If the track switch does not snap quickly from one route to the other, the problem is probably a lack of voltage. Remove any locomotives or illuminated cars from the track and try the switch again. If it is still slow, there may be a loose connection in the rails somewhere on the layout, so move the Lockon and wires to a track section next to the switch and try again.

2. There may be debris around the moving switch points. Clean the debris, and if the switch is still slow, disassemble it and clean the internal working components as shown in this chapter.

WIRING FOR OPERATION

Chapter 6

L ionel Trains are the simplest of all model railroad products to operate and connect to their electrical source. The third rail simplifies wiring, since only two wires are needed, and the challenge of electrical grounding is not nearly as complex as with two rail track. No matter how complicated your railroad becomes, the Lionel system makes it easy. Even if you run a dozen trains on the same track at once, TrainMaster Command Control will allow you to run them all with just two wires to the track.

RUNNING A RAILROAD WITH ELECTRICITY

Nearly all Lionel trains ever made are designed to be operated with 18-volt AC (alternating current). An

The Lionel three-rail system and Lionel TrainMaster Command Control automated train control systems make it easy to run a complex model railroad like Larry LaJambe's spectacular layout.

The Lionel electrical system includes a power pack or transformer (right) to reduce a 115-volt current to 18 volts; a controller (top) to provide speed, direction, and sound control; and the Lockon (bottom) to connect the controller to the track.

electrical device called a rheostat controls the speed of most Lionel locomotives. The rheostat is inside the Lionel transformer and connected to a knob or lever that you move to increase or decrease the speed of the locomotive. When you move the knob or lever to increase the speed, more electrical current is supplied to the rails, which is picked up by the locomotive's wheels and third-rail roller. It is disguised to look like a throttle, so when you "pour on the juice," the train responds with increased speed. The current is carried to the electric motor hidden inside the locomotive's body. As the throttle control opens up, more power reaches the motor, and it revolves faster. This drives the gear that is attached to the axle, which turns the wheels faster to increase the locomotive's speed.

Lionel locomotives are equipped with an electronic reversing unit, which controls the direction of the

The Lionel Visitors Center layout is controlled from this massive panel. There are three 275-watt ZW transformers from the 1950 to 1966 era; two new ZW transformers, each with 360 watts (from four Powerhouses); one TrainMaster Command Base; a TrainMaster CAB-1 remote controller.

motor's armature. As the armature reverses direction, so does the locomotive. There is a feature on the transmission that is like the neutral gear on an automobile that allows the train to be fully powered while standing still.

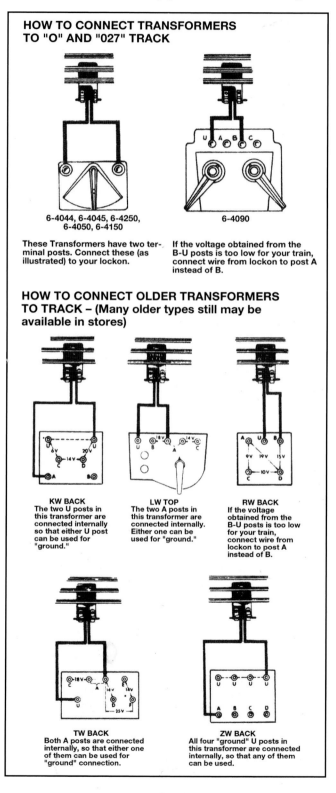

HOW TO CONNECT TRANSFORMERS TO "O" AND "027" TRACK

6-4044, 6-4045, 6-4250, 6-4050, 6-4150

6-4090

These Transformers have two terminal posts. Connect these (as illustrated) to your lockon.

If the voltage obtained from the B-U posts is too low for your train, connect wire from lockon to post A instead of B.

HOW TO CONNECT OLDER TRANSFORMERS TO TRACK – (Many older types still may be available in stores)

KW BACK
The two U posts in this transformer are connected internally so that either U post can be used for "ground."

LW TOP
The two A posts in this transformer are connected internally. Either one can be used for "ground."

RW BACK
If the voltage obtained from the B-U posts is too low for your train, connect wire from lockon to post A instead of B.

TW BACK
Both A posts are connected internally, so that either one of them can be used for "ground" connection.

ZW BACK
All four "ground" U posts in this transformer are connected internally, so that any of them can be used.

Everytime you bring your throttle to zero or push the reversing button on the transformer for a second, you will cycle through this sequence: forward, neutral, reverse, neutral, forward, and so on. It allows you total control of your locomotive's operations. Using the lockout switch on select locomotives, you can program your train to run in only one direction, usually forward in the case of multi-engine lash-ups or in operations using reversing loops. For more sophisticated operations using TrainMaster Command Control, you can program your locomotive to operate without neutral.

Lionel offers a variety of step-down transformers that reduce the common household 110 volts down to 18 volts. Lionel also offers many controllers to regulate the speed and direction of the locomotive and activate the whistle, bell, or horn. Some Lionel control systems have a separate box or transformer to convert electrical current from 110 to 18 volts with a separate plug-in controller to provide speed; a button for forward/reverse; and a second button to actuate whistle, bell, and RailSounds.

Lionel also offers the powerful CW-80, an 80-watt transformer, which incorporates the transformer function, speed, forward/reverse, and sound-activation buttons into a single case.

If you have massive locomotives requiring more pulling power, Lionel's top-of-the-line control system is the ZW controller with two separate plug-in PowerHouse 180-watt transformers for a total of 360 watts of power. You can run up to four trains with the ZW and four massive throttle levers. The ZW, like most Lionel transformers, can also be used to provide power for the TrainMaster Command Control system.

MAKING THE CONNECTIONS

On most Lionel transformers, there are two posts or terminals to be connected with two wires to the Lockon on the track, or to the FasTrack terminal track. With some of the larger transformers, there may be four or more posts. The extra pairs of posts are designed to provide a fixed or variable current for accessories, in addition to the two posts to supply variable voltage to the track. The instruction manual furnished with each transformer will help you determine which terminals or posts are intended to supply power for the track and which are for accessories. The chart and the diagrams illustrate some typical terminal arrangements for older Lionel transformers, including the classic Postwar ZW (the current ZW has different terminals from that of the older version).

Transformer	With this as Common or Ground Post	These are the Fixed Voltage Posts		And these are the Variable Voltage Posts	
1032, 1033, 1044 Multi-Control 90 Watts	A	C B	16 V. 5 V.	U	5-16 V.
	B	C	11 V.	U	0-11 V.
	C	A B	16 V. 11 V.	None	
	U	None		A B	5-16 V. 0-11 V.
'KW' Multi-Control 190 Watts	U	D C	20 V. 6 V.	A B	6-20 V. 6-20 V.
	C	D U	14 V. 6 V.	A B	0-14 V. 0-14 V.
'LW' Multi-Control 125 Watts	A	B C	18 V. 14 V.	U	6-20 V.
'VW', 'ZW' Multi-Control	U	None * With Internal Whistle Control		A* B C D*	6-20 V. 6-20 V. 6-20 V. 6-20 V.
'TW' Multi-Control 175 Watts	A	C D B	18 V. 14 V. 7 V.	U	7-18
	B	A	7 V.	U	0-11
	In additon this transformer has 2 posts marked E and F which furnish an independent 14V source to supply lights, accessories, etc.				
'A', 'Q'	A	C B	14 V. 8 V.	U	14-24 V.
	B	A C	8 V. 6 V.	U	16-6 V.
	U	None		A B	14-24 V. 6-16 V.
'R'	A	D B	14 V. 8 V.	C F	14-24 V. 14-24 V.
	B	E A	16 V. 8 V.	C F	6-16 V. 6-16 V.
	D	A E	14 V. 10 V.	None	
'RW' Multi-Control	A	D C	19 V. 9 V.	U	9-19 V.
	B	D C	16 V. 6 V.	U	6-16 V.
	D	A B C	19 V. 16 V. 10 V.	None	

(chart continued on next page)

Transformer	With this as Common or Ground Post	These are the Fixed Voltage Posts		And these are the Variable Voltage Posts	
'V', 'Z'	U	None		A	6-25 V.
				B	6-25 V.
				C	6-25 V.
				D	6-25 V.
Postwar 'ZW' 135/80 Watts	U	None		A	4-18 V.
				B	4-18 V.
				C	4-18 V.
				D	4-18 V.
'BW', 'CW' 80 Watts	U	B	12 V.	A	4-18 V.
				B	4-18 V.

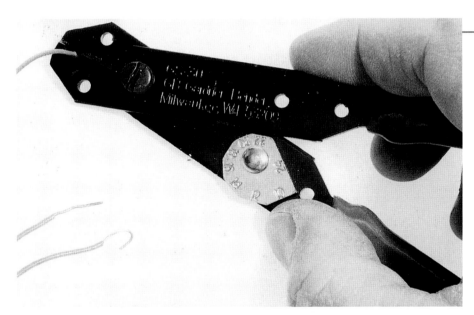

Use wire strippers to remove the insulation from the wires. Twist the loose strands together. If you are connecting the transformer to a screw-style post, form a C-shaped loop in the wire (lower right).

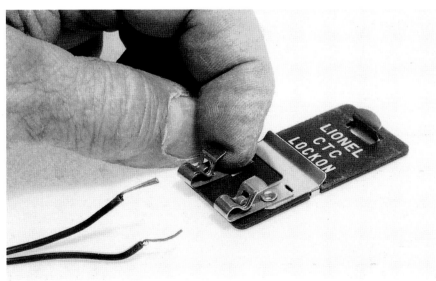

Press down on the Lionel Lockon's clip and insert the bare end of the wire.

Insert the bare wire ends into the spring clips. Make sure the bare ends are at least 1/4 inch apart so they cannot accidentally touch each other.

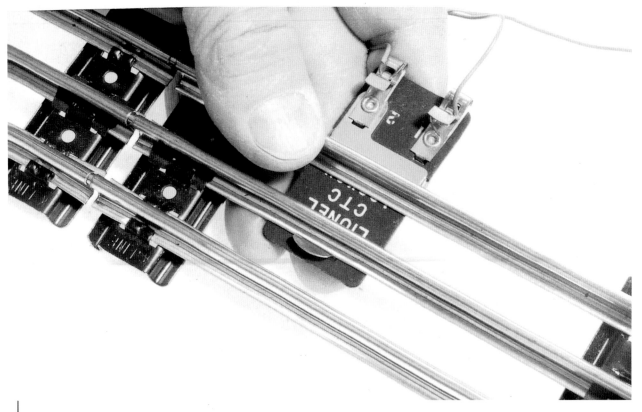

Install the Lockon by pressing the base of the outer rail into the long metal clip, then pivot the Lockon up to snap the clip over the bottom of the center rail.

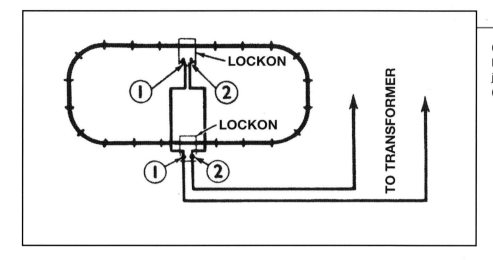

On larger layouts, install a second Lockon on every 6 feet of track with jumper or feeder wires connected (as shown). *Courtesy Lionel LLC*

If your trains run erratically or stop running, there's a good chance the trouble is due to a poor electrical connection. The proper way to make an electrical connection is to strip the insulation off 3/8th of an inch at the wire's end. The insulation alone should be removed without nicking the copper wires, and you'll want to have a wire-stripper tool sold by most hardware stores, electronics stores, and hobby shops. Determine the size of the wire (the shop can help) and set the adjustment on the wire stripper to the correct number. You should then be able to simply clamp down on the insulation with the wire stripper until the jaws bottom out and pull the wire through the jaws, leaving the 3/8th of an inch of insulation behind. Practice with a length of scrap wire until you get it right. It takes some practice to perfect this technique.

With the insulation removed, twist the loose strands together like a miniature rope. These pigtail ends can be inserted into the spring tabs on the Lockon. If you are going to attach the wires to screw-type terminals like those on Lionel switches, bend the bare end of the wire around a screwdriver handle to form a C-shaped end for better contact. With FasTrack, you will find the situation is reversed. The wires are permanently attached to the terminal track and must be inserted into the terminal posts on the transformer, and the terminal nuts tightened to secure them.

When you attach the wires to the track or a transformer, make sure there is no possible way for the bare wires from one terminal or post to touch another. If the exposed ends are too long, cut them off with scissors or a wire cutter. When wires touch one another, they short circuit the system and prevent the transformer from functioning.

The three rails carry the current around the layout. With each track joint there is a minor electrical power loss that can result in slightly less power when the train is over 12 feet from the connection to the transformer. On large layouts, you can ensure smooth operation all around the track by running a pair of jumper wires every 6 feet or so around the layout. When using Lockons (O-27 and O Gauge), be sure that the wire from post 1 on the first Lockon also goes to post 1 on the second Lockon, and that the wire from post 2 is also connected to the second Lockon's post 2. You can add a third Lockon by connecting another pair of wires from the second Lockon and so on. If you use FasTrack, you have the option of using terminal tracks, space lugs, or soldering to jumper your connection to the track. Just be sure to connect the wire powering the outside rails to the same terminal with every jumper you add. It's pretty easy if you look at the bottom of the FasTrack and observe how the contacts are wired. If you are dividing the layout into electrically insulated blocks, the wiring connections will need to include an on-off switch, as shown in Chapter 8.

LIONEL TRAINMASTER COMMAND CONTROL

The gem of Lionel train control options is TrainMaster Command Control (TMCC). With TMCC, a single handheld CAB-1 remote control that looks like a television remote, is used to control the locomotive. You can use the TrainMaster CAB-1 remote as a handheld controller to run one locomotive at a time, even if your layout has no locomotives or accessories fitted with TMCC receiver units. Just as with conventional operation, you will still need a power supply with at least 18 volts (a large Lionel transformer or a Lionel PowerHouse power supply), the TrainMaster PowerMaster pack or Track Power Controller

(TPC) 300, a Command Base, and the CAB-1 Remote Controller. In other words, these are all the components you need to run several TrainMaster-equipped locomotives and accessories. At this point, since you have all the components, why not try a few TrainMaster Command Control-equipped locomotives? You can run dozens of locomotives, all at the same time, from that same CAB-1 remote, as described in Chapter 7. Builders note: If you aren't sure you want to jump to TMCC, the Conventional Command Center (C^3)provides all of the best operating and sound features of TMCC without having to become an electronics expert. With a C^3, you can be a basic operator while it converts your commands into technical strings of operations that your layout will execute for you. Best of all, when you graduate into full-fledged TMCC operation, your C^3 will play the role of the command base, so it never becomes obsolete.

The TMCC system is really like a kind of magic wand in your hand. You can walk anywhere in the room with the CAB-1 and control the entire layout. Walk along beside the locomotive or sit back in an easy chair and play Master of the Universe. The Cab-1 remote will control any locomotive you choose at any time and will activate any of the RailSounds anywhere on the layout. The CAB-1 also activates uncoupling tracks, and for car and locomotives equipped with ElectroCouplers, it will uncouple the cars anywhere on the track. The control buttons on the CAB-1 also allow you to operate any accessory, and you can program a sequence of train operations to command the train to work through an alternate route each time around the layout. Some of these functions require additional TMCC components.

HOW TRAINMASTER COMMAND CONTROL WORKS

When Lionel's TMCC is used with TMCC-equipped locomotives, a steady 18 volts is fed to the rails through a carefully regulated electrical system. The speed control is actually inside the locomotive while the track is always at full power. The handheld CAB-1 sends a radio signal command, such as speed up or slow down to the command base, which digitizes the signal and transmits it through the track's outside rails. An antennae in the locomotive (often it's one of the handrails) receives the radio signals,

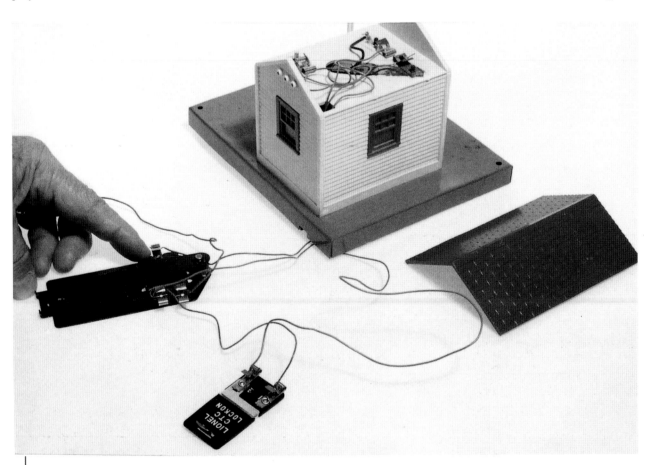

The 153C Contactor is placed beneath the track, and the Lockon is clipped to the track.

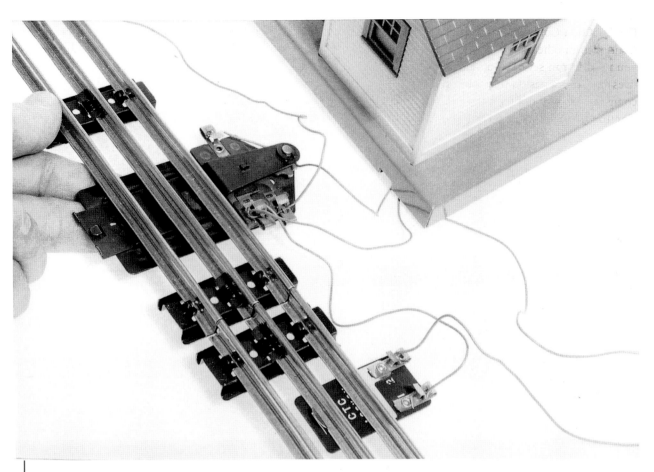

Connect the wires from the accessory or crossing signal (this is Lionel's Automatic Gateman) to the 153C Connector as shown. This accessory receives its power from a Lockon on the track. It is better to connect the wires directly to a separate transformer dedicated to accessories.

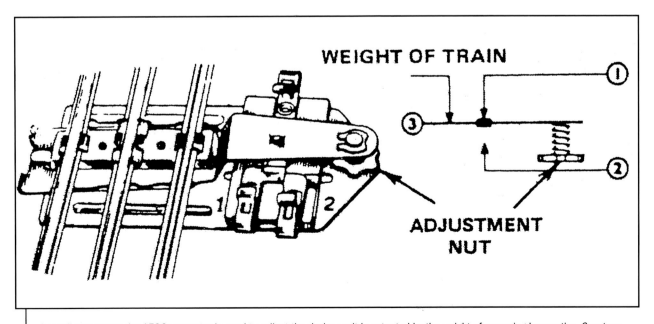

WEIGHT OF TRAIN

ADJUSTMENT NUT

A small star nut on the 153C contactor is used to adjust the device so it is actuated by the weight of a passing locomotive. *Courtesy Lionel LLC*

and the engine's TMCC electronics then process and respond to the transmitted command.

The HO and N scale trains use a system called Digital Command Control (DCC), which uses the rails to send the commands to the receiver. The handheld controller is connected to the track by wires, unless a separate radio control station is installed to receive the signals trackside. Lionel TMCC is a simpler system that requires very little wiring. If you already have a Lionel layout, you can install TMCC by connecting one additional wire.

As time passes, TMCC is updated to make it versatile for all new technical developments in the model railroad hobby. See your dealer or visit the website for the latest in TMCC.

WIRING ACCESSORIES

Most Lionel accessories are designed to use a fixed voltage. Most of the medium-sized and large Lionel transformers are equipped with a second pair of posts for accessories. The voltage for accessories varies by the transformer, and the most common Lionel transformers are shown in the chart, along with the letters that identify which pairs of posts provide which voltage. If your transformer does not have fixed-voltage terminals, you can add a second unit and turn the voltage up just enough to supply the accessory's requirements. You can also purchase a transformer specifically designed for Lionel accessories

with 36 watts of variable power. I recommend that you obtain a separate power supply for accessories and another power supply for switches so the operation of the accessories and switches does not affect the operation of the trains. Builders note: Remember that with FasTrack switches, their power draw is so efficient that you can run them off track power.

TRAIN-ACTUATED SIGNALS AND CROSSING GATES

Lionel offers a range of signals and crossing gates to match most of those seen on real railroads. Lionel has offered dozens of two-bulb searchlight signals and drop-arm semaphore signals over the years, both in Postwar and scale (mainline) sizes.

Some of the Lionel signals and crossing warning devices are supplied with a Lionel 153C contactor, a simple contact switch that is actuated by the weight of the train, which closes a circuit that activates the accessory. Lionel has offered dozens of variations on each of these devices over the years, and your choices at any given time are numerous.

The Lionel 153C contactor is what tells the signal lights or crossing warning devices to light up or move. The 153C consists of a pair of metal plates held apart by a spring. The weight of the train compresses the spring so the metal plates touch to complete an electrical circuit

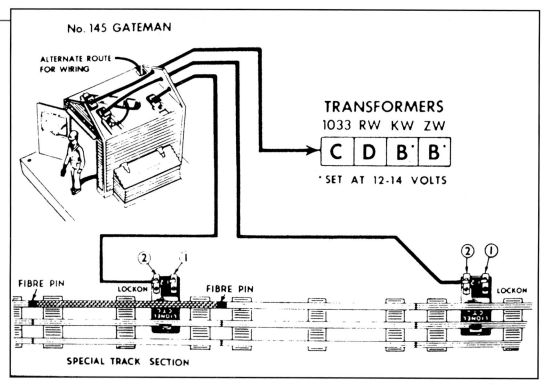

You can substitute a Lionel Insulated Track Section for the 153C contactor by installing the track section to actuate signals or accessories like the Automatic Gateman. *Courtesy Lionel LLC*

No. 145 GATEMAN

ALTERNATE ROUTE FOR WIRING

TRANSFORMERS
1033 RW KW ZW

C D B∙ B∙

∙SET AT 12-14 VOLTS

FIBRE PIN

LOCKON

FIBRE PIN

LOCKON

SPECIAL TRACK SECTION

to turn on the signal or crossing warning device. The 153C should be adjusted precisely, using the replacement nut, to match the weight of your locomotive.

You may choose to provide each Lionel signal or crossing-warning device with its own power. Using a separate transformer assures that the accessory will not affect the operation of the trains (and vice versa). You may want to group several together, powered by a transformer, and assign these groups by physical proximity or function. For example, a coal ramp and a coal loader could be powered by one transformer, even though the ramp is across the layout from the coal loader. If you choose to use track power, you can pick up power from O and O-27 gauge track using a Lockon, as shown in the photographs. Similarly you can pick up power from FasTrack by running wires from the lugs on the underside of any track section. If you have a separate power supply, the two wires connected to the Lockon would be connected to the terminal posts on the power supply. One of the power wires goes to the accessory, and one goes to the terminal on the 153C, as shown in the wiring diagram furnished with the accessory. Two wires lead from the 153C to the accessory. A fourth wire is shown

in the photographs to lead to another signal or crossing gate farther down the track.

Lionel has also supplied other similar contactors in the past, and you may encounter these if you buy a vintage accessory. These devices operate on the same principle as the 153C, but the wiring can vary, so always follow the wiring diagram furnished with the accessory and use the contactor suggested on the instruction sheet.

If you are running trains in both directions, you may want to install contactors a foot or so both to the right and left of the signal or crossing warning devices so the device will be actuated properly by trains traveling in either direction.

THE MAGIC OF THREE RAILS: INSULATED TRACK SECTIONS

Three rails provide many advantages such as the ability to use the track as a trigger to control signals and warning devices, like Automatic Gateman, in addition to automatic switch control. With the insulated track section, there is no need for special contacts or electrical switches. Just replace a regular straight section with an insulated track section and you can build a "smart" layout.

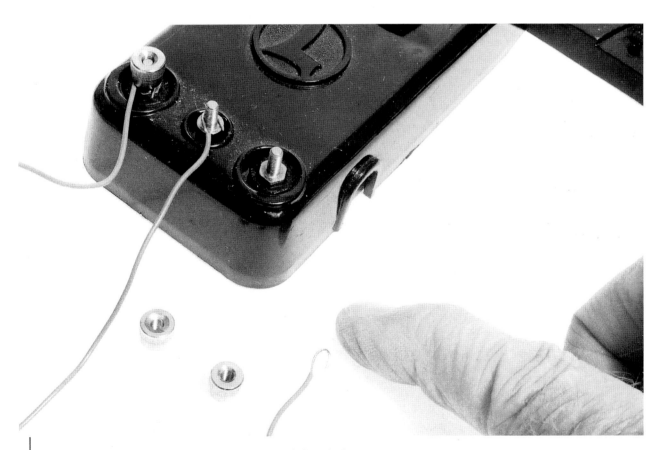

Install the C-shaped bare wire ends and tighten the knurled terminal nuts.

Lionel offers insulated track sections as standard-length straights for O-27, O, and FasTrack. FasTrack uses the Accessory Activator Pack, which is an insulated track with isolated companion sections, to enable the train to trigger accessory operations.

The insulated track section offers an easy way to actuate Lionel signals, crossing warning devices, or track-side accessories. The insulated track section is merely a single piece of track with one of the outside rails insulated from the other outside rail. When you install an O or O-27 insulated track section, fiber pins must be installed in place of the steel pins at both ends of the insulated rail (with the FasTrack Accessory Activator Pack, the insulated pins are already installed). That insulated outside rail can now serve as a contactor to activate any warning accessory. The passing of the locomotive (or cars) closes the circuit between the power from the third rail and the power from the electrically isolated rail. Because both outside rails provide the same electrical power, one of those rails is free to be used as an insulated track section without significantly affecting the flow of electricity to the locomotive.

To install the O and O-27 insulated track section, replace the standard straight piece of track with the insulated track section and install a fiber pin at both ends of the insulated rail. In place of the 153C contactor, install a Lockon clipped to the insulated outside and center rail. For some devices, like the crossing Automatic Gateman, two Lockons are needed on the unmodified rails of the track sections on either side of the insulated rail. This leaves no electrical connection to the insulated track section. The passing locomotive provides a connection between the insulated rail and the first Lockon to turn on the device, and a second contact between the second Lockon and the insulated rail turns off the device. There are no moving parts. All you need are clean rails, which is a regular operating requirement. Builders note: If you are handy, you can make your own O and O-27 insulated track section by removing one outside rail and inserting tough thin fiber (non-conductive) insulators between the rail and the ties, just as Lionel does. You might want to build your own insulated track section if you require one for a curved track section because Lionel only offers straight insulated track sections. To operate properly, the insulated track section must be the full length of a straight or curved track section.

The convenient FasTrack Accessory Activator Pack includes everthing you need to activate your single operation, on-or-off accessories. Two isolated track sections feature gaps that break the flow of electricity to the outside rail. An insulated track section is place between these sections to make the isolated section longer. The accessory is attached to the insulated track section via an accessory wire, which is already attached to the track. Connect an accessory to the bare ends of the wire, and you are ready for operation.

CONTROL BY INFRARED LIGHT BEAM

Lionel offers the 153IR controller (6-14111), a third option to control signals and accessories. It looks like a trackside maintenance shed, but it houses an infrared beam and sensor, along with a timer that can be adjusted to allow a 0 to 20 second time delay. The 153IR sends out a beam that, when broken, triggers an accessory to function for a variable length of time. It is the most reliable contactor out there and it is easy to install. You don't need to attach any special devices to the track or use special track sections. Just attach the 153IR controller to ends of the ties or to the contacts built into the ballast of FasTrack, and run the wires to the signal or crossing gate and to the transformer. The 153IR is the simplest method of controlling signals, but on a layout with dozens of signals, you may want to alternate between installations of the 153IR and the insulated track sections, especially if you want the signal or other accessory to be actuated by trains traveling in either direction.

WIRING SWITCHES

Lionel offers manual and remote-controlled O-27 switches in each of its three track systems: manual and remote control 27- and 42-inch diameter remote-control in O-27; 31- and 72-inch diameter in O Gauge; and manual or remote-control 36- or 72-inch remote-control and 72-inch diameter wye switch, with more configurations in the works. All remote switches are designed to be manually operated, but manual switches can't be made into a remote control switch.

The remote-control switches can pick up their power from the rails, or you can supply a separate power source from the fixed-voltage outlets on the main track transformer or on a transformer dedicated specifically to your switches.

The O-27, O-42, O Gauge, and 0-72 switches include an operating lever with three wires. The operating levers are integrated into the switch control boxes, as shown in the instructions. To install the wires, strip the insulation from about 3/8-inch of the ends of the wires and bend the bare ends into C-shaped loops. Loop the wire around the control posts with the ends facing the right so that when the knurled nut on the switch control box is tightened, it pulls the wire tighter around the post.

The switches can also be wired to be actuated by the trains. You can provide an automatic alternate routing over two sidings like track A and track B in the diagram by connecting the center terminals with one jumper or feeder wire and the inside terminals with a second jumper wire, as shown in the diagram.

Lionel switches (turnouts) have a built-in feature to prevent trains from being derailed when they arrive at the switch from a diverging route and if the switch set for the wrong direction. The incoming train will automatically throw the switch points to the correct route. Before entering the switch, thus preventing a derailment, is the non-derailing feature. To activate the non-derailing feature, you must install insulated fiber pins in place of the steel pins on the appropriate rails. The insulated pins come packed with a switch. The instructions that come with the switches explain where this feature is and how it works.

You may discover that some locomotives that have rubber traction tires do not activate the non-derailing feature quickly enough to avoid derailments. This is quite rare, but with longer wheelbase modern diesels, it could happen. What it means is that the fiber pins must be located at least a half-section of track in advance of the switch. To accomplish this, replace the fiber pins in the two rails at the switch with steel pins. Attach the new track sections to the two diverging routes of the switch in the normal manner, but one of the steel track pins at the end of each of the two track sections leading out from the switch must be replaced with fiber pins. Replace the pin in the appropriate rails closest to one another in each track section. Essentially, you are leap-frogging the fiber pins one track section out from the switch to provide the additional length of track needed to activate the non-derailing feature in time. Builders note: Do not do this until you notice a problem with derailments of locomotives going into a switch against two switch points. It is very rare, and should only affect your trains if you are driving them at high speeds. High-speed racing through switches can cause derailments all by itself. Remember to slow down when you approach a switch if you have a heavy throttle hand.

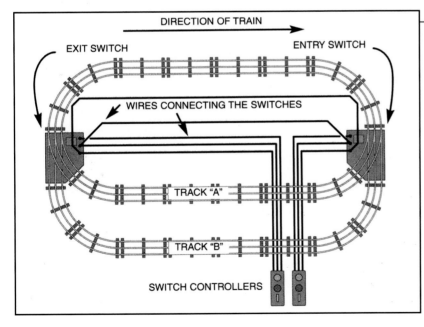

If you connect the wires to the Lionel switches and install the fiber pins into the indicated rails of each switch, the trains will automatically alternate between Track A and Track B each time around the oval. *Courtesy Lionel LLC*

The four rectangular boxes are the remote-control switch operating levers, and the push-button switches actuate accessories on Robert Babas' layout.

Chapter 7

TWO-TRAIN OPERATIONS

With today's technology, you can operate dozens of Lionel locomotives on a single track. The trick is to provide a means of independent control for each locomotive and be able to multi-task sufficiently to actually keep track of them all while you are operating them.

There are really three choices. The simplest is to create a separate loop of track for each train and provide each train with its own transformer. This is easy to build and easy to operate, but the trains can't interact with one another. The second method is to use TMCC to provide power and direction for the layout. TMCC provides completely independent control for each of dozens of locomotives to be operated at the same time on the same track. It is easy to install, learn, and operate, but it can be a little daunting at first. The most complex method,

Even with toy trains like Thomas the Tank Engine, you might want to run two trains at once, as on Michael Ulewicz' layout.

but one chosen by many conventional railroaders before they graduate into full-blown TMCC operation, has been in use for nearly a century. The method is to divide the track's rails into electrically isolated blocks so each train occupies only one block.

Understanding blocks is worthwhile no matter which of the applications you choose. Sometimes if you are going to have a train layout, you will encounter a valuable use for blocks.

THE BLOCK SYSTEM FOR TWO-TRAIN OPERATION

It is unlikely you will want to have one train chasing another around a simple oval, so we'll use a more interesting example of an oval with passing siding on one

The Lionel Visitors Center layout is operated with TrainMaster Command Control, so many locomotives can be operated at once.

end. You can park one train on either leg of the passing siding while you operate a second train around the oval. The oval with passing siding must be divided into three blocks so you can park a train on either leg of the passing siding and turn off power to only that portion of the track. You can then run one train at a time and park the second.

Simple on-off toggle switches (SPST) are available for outdoor installation with ceramic bases and rugged components. You can use them for standard block control even for a portable layout on the floor.

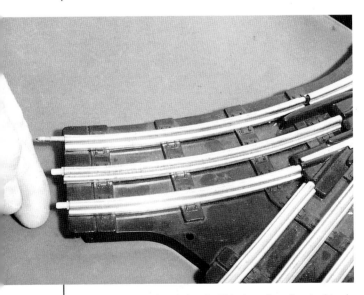

To provide an insulated electrical block, replace the steel track pin in the center rail with a Lionel fiber pin. If the track switch is going to be activated automatically, you will need a second insulated track pin, as described in Chapter 6.

The basic electric components for this simple two-train layout are two on-off switches so you can turn off the power to one siding while you turn on the other. You will also need four fiber track pins to replace the four steel track pins in the third rail. Replace the steel pins in the center rail with Lionel fiber pins for O-27 or O Gauge track depending on what you use on your layout, fiber pins don't carry electrical current. The track diagram shows the locations of the fiber pins as large dots in circled letters A, B, C, and D. You will also need three Lockons, installed as shown with letters W, X, and Y. Use 14- or 16-gauge wire to connect the on-off switches and the Lockons to the transformer. The photo shows the simple wire connections to the three Lockons. You can use the system with much more complicated plans and track arrangements as long as you have some track route for the running train to pass the parked train.

The photo shows a simple set of two on-off switches and the necessary wires. The large white dots indicate where fiber track pins must be inserted. A second pair

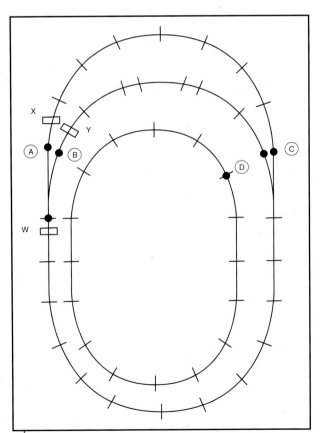

This track diagram is for an oval with passing siding so you can park a train on either leg of the siding. A third train can be operated on the inner oval. The letters A, B, C, and D indicate where fiber pins should be inserted in the third rails; and the letters W, X, and Y are the Lockon/terminal track locations.

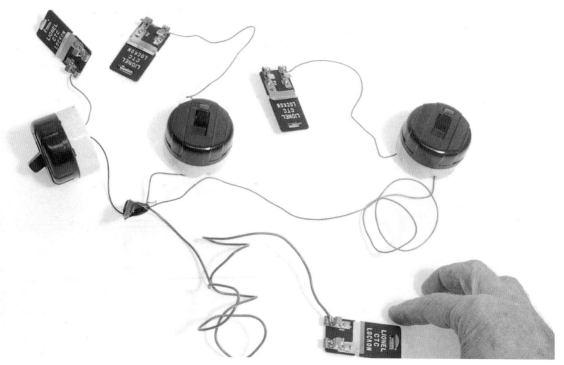

You can create portable wiring, even for a layout on the floor. Here, one wire from the mainline Lockon is joined to three wires from three additional Lockons, each with its own on-off switch. The three block Lockons only have wires to the center rail clips (post number 1). Fiber pins in the center rail are used to divide the layout into three electrically isolated blocks that are controlled by three on-off switches.

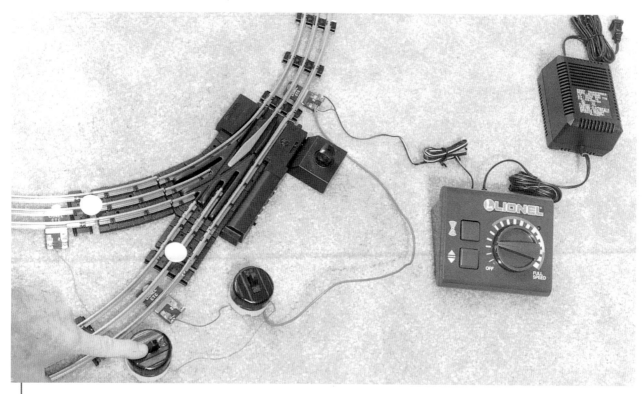

Only two on-off switches are needed for the simple oval with passing siding layout. The white dots indicate where fiber pins are inserted into the third rails (another pair of fiber pins must be inserted in the second switch on the other side of the oval). Both wires from the transformer connect only to the Lockon on the single-track side of the switch (top).

must be inserted in the tracks on the opposite ends of the two sidings. Only three wires need be connected to the track: one from the main Lockon (top) to an on-off switch to control the outside track (center), and another from that switch to a second on-off switch to control the inside track (bottom). To run a train on the outer oval, you would turn the middle on-off switch to "on" and the lower switch to "off." To operate a train on the inner oval, turn the middle switch to "off" and the lower switch to "on." The single transformer is used to control either train since only one train will operate at a time. For FasTrack you must substitute the accessory activator for the fiber pins, and the terminal tracks for the Lockons. Otherwise, the specifications for on/off switches are the same for all track types.

RUNNING TWO TRAINS AT ONCE

This system allows you to run two trains at the same time, each on its own oval with a crossover pair of switches (turnouts) so that either train can cross over into the other train's oval. This is the block wiring system used on the double-oval and the loop-to-loop layouts in Chapter 3. The inner oval is electrically isolated from the outer oval by inserting a single fiber pin between the switches at each crossover. The inner oval has its own on-off electrical switch, and the outer oval is divided into three blocks, each with its own on-off electrical switch. You probably want to use a separate transformer to provide independent speed control for each train. You could replace any on-off switch with a separate transformer. Two transformers, one for the inner

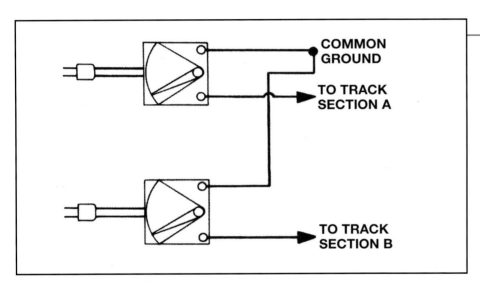

As illustrated in this wiring diagram, be sure the 110-volt plugs (left) and the 18-volt wires (right) from the two transformers are all wired "in phase", as described in the text. *Courtesy Lionel LLC*

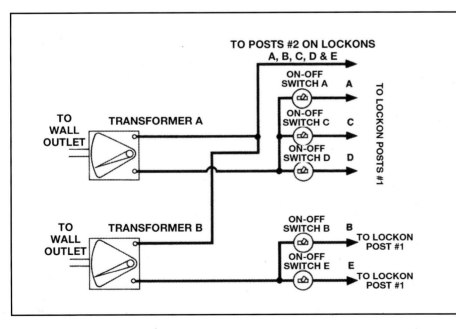

The common ground wires from both transformers are connected to the outside rail clip (post number 2). The second wires from the transformers can be divided to connect any number of blocks with on-off switches (five are shown here: Blocks A, B, C, D, and E). *Courtesy Lionel LLC*

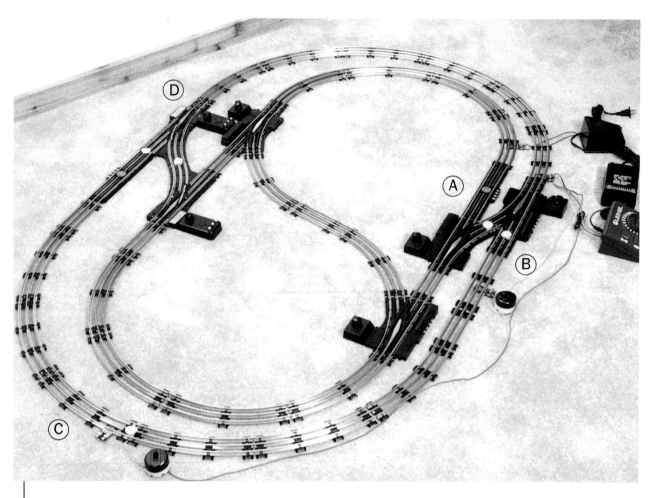

You can use the outdoor-style on-off switches and wires for a temporary layout on the floor. This simple two-oval layout is divided into four blocks with four on-off switches (only two switches are shown here). The inner oval is Block A. The outer oval is divided into three blocks: B, C, and D. The large white dots indicate where fiber track pins are used in the third rails.

and one for the outer oval, will provide enough power for this layout.

If you want to use two transformers to provide independent control for two trains, the transformers must be phased so the common ground wires from both transformers are connected to the outside of each transformer (posts number 2), and the second wires from each transformer are connected to the Lockon's center rail (posts number 1). The two transformers must be wired as shown in the diagram, with the wire to track section A going to the center rail post number 1 on the Lockon for block A, and the wire for track section B going to the center rail post number 1 on the Lockon for block B. The common ground wires should be joined and connected to the outer rail post number 2 on the Lockons for both blocks A and B.

The 115-volt wires leading to the transformers must also be phased. The wires leading to the wall plugs from each transformer must be plugged in with the larger prong from each plug in the righthand hole of the wall socket or extension cord. You can test the system with a Lionel 18-volt streetlight or an 18-volt bulb with bare wire leads. Touch one wire from the light to terminal A on one transformer and to terminal A on the second transformer. If the light glows, the transformers are out of phase. The plugs at the end of either of the transformer's power cord must be pulled out of the walls socket, rotated 180 degrees, and plugged back in. You can mark the plugs and sockets with masking tape to be sure you get them right every time you plug them in. It's a good idea to invest in a power strip with a surge protector to plug in all of the transformers to provide overload protection.

The connections from the two transformers to the Lockons are made following the schematic for transformers A and B with wires to on-off switches A through

E (although for this simple two-oval example, you will only need blocks A, B, C, and D).

The track must be modified slightly to operate two trains at once. The first step is to install insulating fiber pins between each pair of switches to electrically isolate the inner oval (block A) from the outer oval (blocks B, C and D) at the dots marked with circled letters A and E on the photo. If you want to move the train from the inner oval (train 2), you will need to park the train on the outer oval (train 1). You will then need a third electrically isolated block to be able to park train 1 and a fourth electrically isolated block to park train 2. Three more fiber pins will need to be installed, as indicated by the dots and circled letters B, C, and D, to divide the left half of the outer oval into two blocks, the original block B and third and fourth blocks C and D. As with the earlier example, FasTrack enables you to accomplish the same techniques by adding an insulated track section at each point you see fiber pins being called for. Also, you will use a terminal track at each point where we designate an O and O-27.

TWO TRAINS AND MORE WITH THE ZW

I've shown two Lionel train set transformers controlling double-oval trains. Lionel also offers the massive ZW, complete with two 180-watt PowerHouse transformers, which can control up to four trains. The ZW is programmed so that track 1 is controlled by the A handle, track 2 by the B handle, track 3 by the C handle, and track 4 by the D handle.

The ZW transformer can also be used as a power source for the Lionel TMCC, which is shown in this chapter. If you use TMCC, you can use the handheld CAB-1 remote unit to control both trains and more.

LOOP-TO-LOOP OPERATIONS FOR THREE TRAINS

On the loop-to-loop layout, each reverse loop is divided into two blocks. The photo shows the wires with large white dots on the center rail to indicate where insulating fiber pins are needed, but only the on-off block switches are shown. The transformers and their wires are not represented. For this loop-to-loop layout, five blocks are needed, two for each of the reverse loops and one for the

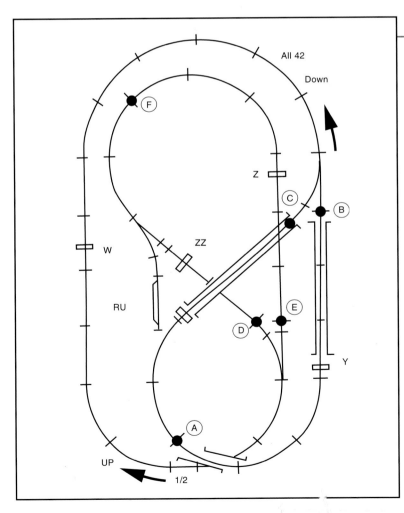

The track plan for the loop-to-loop layout with large dots and the letters A, B, C, D, E, and F indicate where fiber pins are inserted into the third rail joints. The other C and S letters are the small curved track sections. If you are using Lionel's conventional 0 Gauge switches, tracks C and S are built into each switch.

This is the loop-to-loop layout for Chapter 3 with the locations for the fiber pins in the third rail marked with white dots. The on-off switches to control blocks X, Y, Z, and ZZ are installed. The transformer will control the mainline block W.

mainline. The wiring diagram (shown on page 95) for two transformers shows how the five blocks can be connected to the two transformers. Since only two of the three trains will be operating at any one time, two transformers will be enough for the loop-to-loop layout.

When train 1 enters the upper-level reverse loop, it runs almost all the way around and stops just short of the switch. The block that controls half of the reverse loop should be turned off so train 2 can run up behind train 1 and be parked by turning off the switch that controls the second half (the block) of the reverse loop. The block beneath train 1 can then be turned on, and train 1 can proceed out of the reverse loop and back on the mainline towards the second reversing loop. Train 2 can then be moved to the block previously occupied by train 1. Since there is a reverse loop at both ends of this loop-to-loop layout, a third train (train 3) can be parked in the second half of the lower reverse loop to await the arrival of train 1. Train 3 can then proceed onto the mainline and park behind train 2. This musical chairs sequence of running just one train at a time while the other two are parked can be repeated indefinitely with three trains.

TRAINMASTER COMMAND CONTROL

With TMCC, none of the electrically isolating blocks are necessary. Two trains can operate on the double oval or three trains can operate on the loop-to-loop layout, each under completely independent control . On that loop-to-loop layout, train 1 can actually follow just a few inches (or feet) behind train 2, and train 3 can do the same behind train 2 all around the layout. You only have to make sure that two trains don't pass through the switches (turnouts) at the same time and run into one another. That is the real thrill of TMCC: you are running trains, not controlling the track, which is precisely how real railroad engineers, yard masters, and dispatchers runs their trains. Train operation is breathtakingly realistic with the TMCC system.

The controller (a CAB-1 remote controller) for the TMCC system is a wireless remote control unit just a bit larger than a typical television remote control, but it has fewer buttons. Since there are no wires, you can walk along beside your train or sit back in an easy chair and run the layout from the tower. This CAB-1 remote has a knob to control speed; directional, horn and bell buttons;

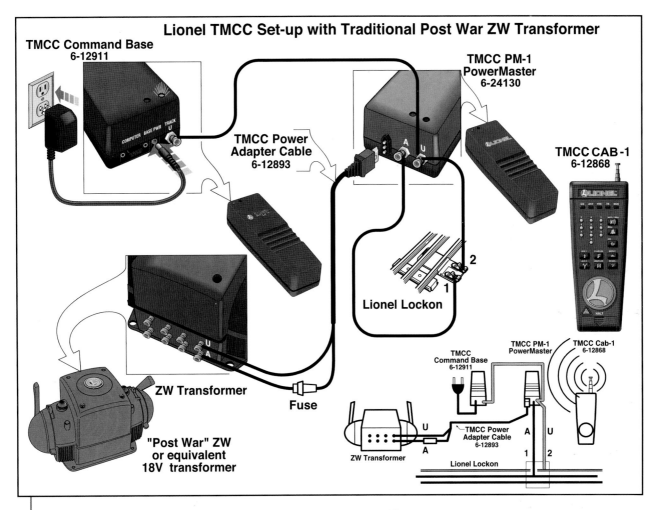

Lionel TMCC Set-up with Traditional Post War ZW Transformer

TMCC Command Base
6-12911

TMCC Power Adapter Cable
6-12893

TMCC PM-1 PowerMaster
6-24130

TMCC CAB-1
6-12868

Lionel Lockon

ZW Transformer

Fuse

"Post War" ZW or equivalent 18V transformer

Lionel TMCC setup with traditional Postwar ZW transformer. *Courtesy Lionel LLC*

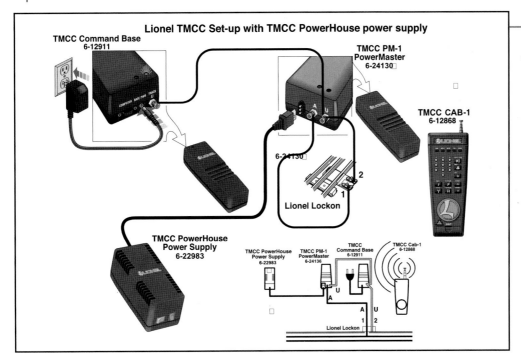

Lionel TMCC Set-up with TMCC PowerHouse power supply

TMCC Command Base
6-12911

TMCC PM-1 PowerMaster
6-24130

TMCC CAB-1
6-12868

6-24130

Lionel Lockon

TMCC PowerHouse Power Supply
6-22983

Lionel TMCC setup with TMCC PowerHouse power supply. *Courtesy Lionel LLC*

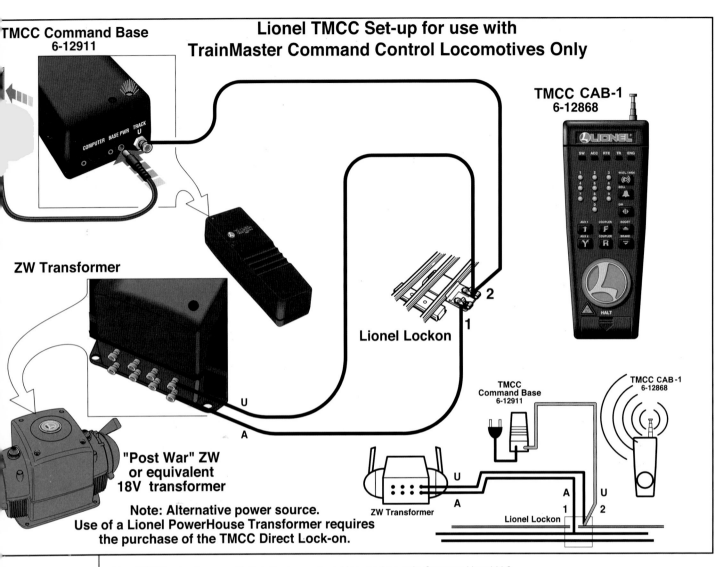

Lionel TMCC Set-up for use with TrainMaster Command Control Locomotives Only

TMCC Command Base 6-12911

TMCC CAB-1 6-12868

ZW Transformer

Lionel Lockon

"Post War" ZW or equivalent 18V transformer

Note: Alternative power source. Use of a Lionel PowerHouse Transformer requires the purchase of the TMCC Direct Lock-on.

TMCC Command Base 6-12911

TMCC CAB-1 6-12868

ZW Transformer

Lionel Lockon

Lionel TMCC setup for use with TrainMaster-equipped locomotives only. *Courtesy Lionel LLC*

auxiliary buttons to activate special sounds, control smoke output, and sound volume; and a set of numbered buttons so you can dial up the number of each locomotive operating car, accessory, or switch you want to control. For potential emergencies, if you are running more trains than you can control, a halt button is available, which stops every TMCC product on the layout.

If you want to run two diesels back-to-back in what the real railroads call multiple-unit lash-ups (mu, for short), you can program each of the locomotives to perform exactly like its mate. The two can then be coupled together, and the TMCC system will keep them operating at identical speeds relative to one another so when

one speeds up, the other matches it precisely. You can also program the locomotives for a longer duration of acceleration or braking to simulate heavier loads. This can be increased to work with several diesels or steamers in a lash-up setting.

Locomotives and cars equipped with Lionel ElectroCouplers can be uncoupled anywhere on the track at the push of a button on the CAB-1. For conventional Lionel operating couplers, the CAB-1 can be used to actuate the uncoupling track or remote-control track to uncouple cars or locomotives on these track sections (or to activate automatic cars that dump or have other animations).

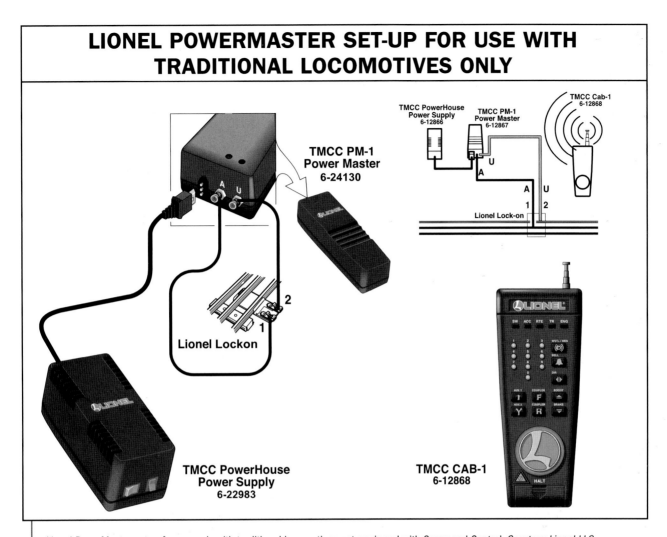

LIONEL POWERMASTER SET-UP FOR USE WITH TRADITIONAL LOCOMOTIVES ONLY

TMCC PM-1 Power Master 6-24130

Lionel Lockon

TMCC PowerHouse Power Supply 6-22983

TMCC PowerHouse Power Supply 6-12866

TMCC PM-1 Power Master 6-12867

TMCC Cab-1 6-12868

Lionel Lock-on

TMCC CAB-1 6-12868

Lionel PowerMaster setup for use only with traditional locomotives not equipped with Command Control. *Courtesy Lionel LLC*

You have full control, through the Lionel RailSounds sound system, of steam locomotive whistles, bells, and exhaust sounds; and diesel locomotive horns, bells, and engine growl sounds using either the CAB-1 or fully equipped conventional Lionel transformers. With TMCC, all locomotive sounds, whether you have a 1950s air whistle or a full RailSounds sound system, are fully accessible. Your transformer can trigger the bells, whistles, diesel roar and horns, but some of RailSounds' most realistic enhancements can only be unleashed via the TMCC system. The amazing potential of your entire Lionel empire is at your fingertips thanks to TMCC and its CAB-1 Remote Controller.

HOW THE TRAINMASTER COMMAND CONTROL SYSTEM WORKS

The TMCC supplies a steady 18 volts to the track rails. Speed control is handled inside the locomotive. The system uses a radio frequency to tell the receiver inside the command base that sends out commands to each locomotive on the entire layout. The command base will make each TMCC-equipped locomotive to speed up, slow down, or reverse. The TMCC system is controlled by a single handheld CAB-1 Remote Controller. The command base created a field that envelops the track within the field. Within the field are the commands that are being issued many times each second to every TMCC locomotive and trackside control unit. An antenna inside each locomotive (in some cases, the handrails serve as an antenna) and the outside track rails relay the signals to the electronics inside the locomotive.

There are five basic components to the Lionel TrainMaster Command Control system:

1. A locomotive or other device equipped with a built-in TrainMaster Command Control receiver.
2. A power supply with at least 18 volts (a large Lionel transformer).
3. A TrainMaster PowerMaster or Track Power Controller (TPC) 300 or 400.
4. A Command Base.
5. The CAB-1 Remote Controller.

The wiring diagrams show how to connect a conventional Lionel transformer like the Postwar ZW or the new TrainMaster PowerHouse engine to the track. These components allow you to run the latest TMCC-equipped or any conventional Lionel locomotive from the past 100 years. Virtually every other locomotive Lionel has ever made (and most other brands of locomotives designed for use on AC three-rail track) will run with TMCC.

If you are using the ZW exclusively to provide power for the TrainMaster Command Control system, turn off the ZW when you are done running trains. The next time you start up the system, give the Command Base PowerMaster and any other transformers a few seconds to come online before turning on the ZW.

If your railroad consists strictly of TMCC-equipped locomotives, you don't need the PowerMaster. Just use the wiring diagram shown here with a powerful 18-volt transformer like a Lionel ZW.

If you are operating only traditional Lionel locomotives and none are equipped with TMCC, you can run your trainsl remotely using a PowerMaster and a CAB-1.

If you use a Lionel PowerHouse in place of the pre-TMCC-equipped ZW transformer, you will also need the TMCC Direct Lockon, which has a small equipment shed to house its sophisticated circuit breaker and electronics. Most of us, however, will want to operate some TMCC-equipped and some conventional Lionel locomotives, so regular Lockons are fine. Conversely, any Lionel locomotives equipped with TMCC will also operate with conventional Lionel controls.

The TMCC system requires at least a CW-80 80-watt transformer. If you are operating larger locomotives or running two or more locomotives at the same time, you may need the 180-watt PowerHouse Power Supply, and you may need two of them. Builders note: The PowerHouse Power Supply, by itself, lacks the special

On a large layout, such as Robert Babas', all the TMCC system components to operate his 20x40-foot system are in a small bookshelf. The whole layout can be operated with the single handheld CAB-1 remote (center, red knob) next to a single command base, and two ZW transformers, each powered by two 180-watt PowerHouse power supplies on the lower shelf.

circuit breakers you will need to protect your system, so use the Power Master, Track Power Controller 300, or the Track Power Controller 400 to operate both conventional and TMCC-equipped locomotives on your layout.

If your model railroad is larger than about 5x9 feet, you should divide it into blocks as described earlier for conventional two-train operation. All you need is a simple fiber pin in the center rail at each of the blocks (Accessory Activator Pack for FasTrack layouts) and a Lockon to connect to the TMCC system, as shown in the diagrams. The blocks provide better electrical current flow and it is easier to isolate any short circuits that might occur from a derailed set of wheels when your layout is broken into blocks. You will need a Power Master and a Track Power Controller 300 or 400 for each block.

Among the specialized TMCC-enhanced components Lionel offers is the TMCC Action Recorder Controller (ARC) that allows you to program up to eight repeatable action sequences. You can have a train automatically follow two alternate routes in succession, or have a train stop at a log loader, dump its load of logs, and proceed around the track to be reloaded with logs, all at the touch of one button on the CAB-1 Remote Controller. The ARC will keep the Lionel equipment following the pattern until you take the controls.

If two or more friends want to operate trains at the same time, you can use additional Cab-1 remote controllers for each of their trains. The TMCC system, with all of its varied elements, is widely expandable. The limit is your imagination.

The TrainMaster SC-2 switch controller can be used for automatic signal control like the one on the Single Signal Bridge beside the Rio Grand EMD GP-30 diesel on the Lionel Visitors Center layout.

TRAINMASTER COMMAND CONTROL TO ANIMATE THE ENTIRE LAYOUT

Lionel offers a variety of electronic components for the TMCC system so the CAB-1 can able used to activate different sounds, puffs of simulated steam or smoke, and turn lights on or off, but that just scratches the surface. With trackside control receivers called "controllers," the CAB-1 remote can actuate switches, turn blocks on or off, uncouple cars, activate action cars and accessories, and even increase or decrease the brightness of lights, all with the push of button.

If your layout is controlled by a TMCC system, you can operate the blocks from the buttons on the walk-around CAB-1 by wiring the blocks through the Block Power Controller. The CAB-1 can also be used to control the speed and smoothness of accessories using the Accessory Motor Controller. If you want to set a speed or brightness of an accessory, use the Accessory Voltage Controller. The Operating Track Controller can actuate the remote control uncoupling track to dump loads, activate other operating cars, and operate automatic uncouplers.

TMCC can serve as your robotic helper, function as a third hand when you're operating multiple trains at once, or it can animate your layout so that an entire route of switches throws at the same moment to open the mainline to a high ball express, or all of the Lionelville lights up at the approach of dusk—all conjured up by you and your TMCC.

Troubleshooting Train Master

Symptom: Circuit Breaker pops too often
Use a larger transformer; 80 watts is the bare minimum, but some locomotives can require 135 or 180 watts on larger layouts.

Symptom: Trains slow down on far side of layout
Add additional Lockon connections to the power supply to have a Lockon for every 6 feet of track.

DIRECTION OF TRAIN →

T SWITCH   ENTRY SWITCH

WIRES CONNECTING THE SWITCHES

PART II

TRACK "A"

TRACK "B"

SWITCH CONTROLLERS

Scenery

Chapter 8

PORTABLE SCENERY

Your Lionel train tracks are designed to be easily assembled and disassembled. You can assemble a Lionel layout, add a track here, a switch there, and rearrange the track layout every week if you please.

Some Lionel railroaders prefer to have a permanent layout with permanent track locations and accessories as described in Chapter 6. But they are missing part of the enjoyment of Lionel, the ability to create a new layout with minimum effort.

The scenery discussed in this chapter can be used on the floor because it is as portable as the track itself. You can, however, use these same scenery techniques on a tabletop, as shown in Chapter 9.

THE EARTH IN A ROLL

Felt is the basic element of this portable scenery. You can buy green, beige, or white felt in 6-foot widths at most fabric shops. You can use the green for summer, beige

This 2x4-foot scene is on Larry LaJambe's permanent layout, but the trees, structures, and tunnel portal could be used on a simple 4x8-foot layout.

Thomas the Tank Engine works his way around a simple 4x8-foot oval built by Michael Ulewicz. The loose ballast is not a good idea for portable layouts, but you could substitute Lionel FasTrack with molded-in ballast.

for winter or arid scenes, and the white for snow scenes. The felt looks like grass or weeds. When you want to store the layout, disassemble the track, put the structures in boxes, and roll up the felt

You will need about 20 percent more felt than the length and width of your layout to leave enough material for mountains. If you are covering a 4x7-foot layout, use about 5x9 feet of felt. Any excess can be tucked under or pinned to the underside of a tabletop with thumbtacks.

You can improve the realism of the green felt by adding splotches of brown latex paint. Lay the felt on the floor and use a roller to apply the paint. You can easily create the effect of patches of bare earth among the grass and weeds if you dab the felt with the roller.

I do not recommend using any kind of loose ballast, ground foam, sawdust, or other loose or granular material because they can get inside the locomotives or the switches. If you want the realism of ballasted track, use Lionel FasTrack.

This scene is on a 4x7-foot layout assembled on a living-room floor. The grass is a 5x9-foot piece of green felt.

The basic elements of portable scenery are green felt, some newspaper, and a Styrofoam tunnel.

MOVABLE MOUNTAINS

If you are modeling Kansas, you can lay the felt right on the floor or tabletop before you begin to lay track. If you want some gently rolling hills, crumple some newspapers and tuck them beneath the felt. Keep the hills or mountains a couple of inches away from the track so they don't cause the track to tilt. Lionel dealers usually carry Styrofoam mountains that can be used either on top of or beneath the felt.

Spread the felt over the area of the layout and tuck the newspaper underneath the felt to form the hills.

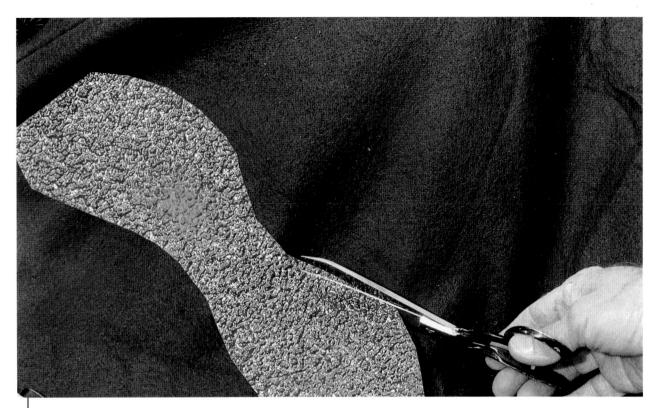

Faller, Kibri, and Noch are three brands of clear plastic water.

Cut the plastic to the shape you desire and lay it on top of the felt.

Cover the edges of the river or lake with clumps of lichen. The joints between pieces of clear plastic water can be covered with bridges.

INSTANT RIVERS AND LAKES

Your Lionel dealer should be able to order clear plastic sheets that have molded ripples to simulate rippling water. Faller, Kibri, and Noch are three choices of clear plastic water sheets your dealer should be able to order for you. You can also crumple and flatten aluminum foil to get a similar effect.

Cut the rippled clear plastic to the shape of the river or lake you desire and lay it on the felt. If you need a longer river, use a second piece of the rippled plastic and hide the joint with a bridge. You can choose from a variety of Lionel bridges for either tracks or highways, so the bridge can carry a road. You can simulate the road with dark gray felt.

Your Lionel dealer should be able to supply lichen, which is Norwegian moss that has been softened in glycerin and dyed green. Shake off any loose bits and place the lichen on the grass mat to simulate bushes. Cover the edges of the rivers or lakes with lichen to provide a more realistic shoreline.

SELF-STANDING TREES

Your Lionel dealer can also order a wide range of free-standing deciduous and coniferous trees. The trees should tower above the trains, so a 7-inch-tall tree is about the minimum size you'd want. Coniferous trees are made from fiber twisted among wires like a toilet brush. Larger pine trees for Lionel layouts include

The larger ready-to-plant coniferous trees include these four (left to right) by Life-Like, Pola, and Noch.

There is a wider choice of deciduous trees including this Life-Like 1971 Giant Oak, Pola 8-inch tree, Pola's 13 7/8-inch tree, and Pola's 14-inch poplar.

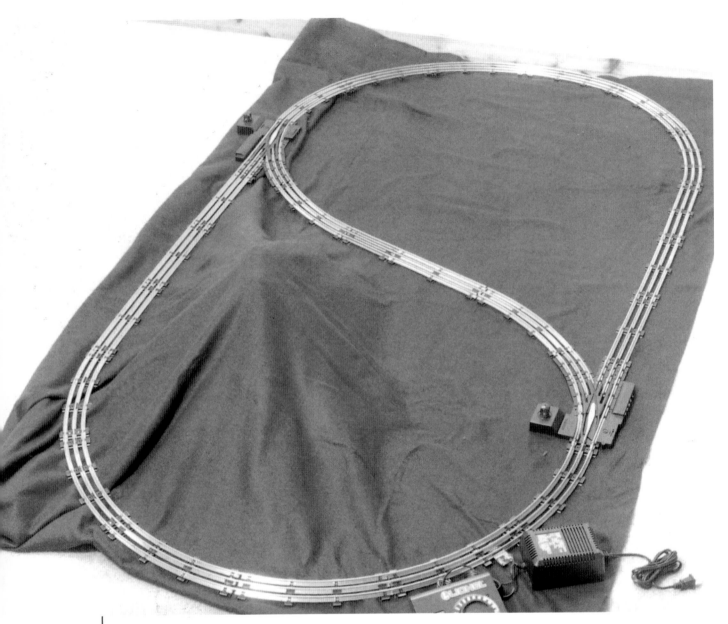

This 4x7-foot oval floor layout with 42-inch diameter outer curves and a reverse loop cutoff is shown in Chapter 3. The edges of the 5x9-foot sheet of felt are tucked underneath.

Life-Like, Pola, and Noch. Model Power also offers a number 1436 assortment of similar trees that are 8 inches tall. You should also be able to find some 10- to 15-inch tall Christmas trees at craft stores.

Deciduous trees are usually made with plastic tree trunks and limbs covered with clumps of lichen or bits of ground foam. My choices include the Life-Like Giant Oak; and Pola's 8-inch tree, 331963 13 7/8-inch tree, and 14-inch poplar. Noch makes an 11 3/4-inch and a 13 3/4-inch birch tree.

FLEXIBLE ROCKS

There may be some areas of your layout where you want to include a rock cliff. The upper-level loop on the two-level layout in Chapter 9 has a rock cliff to hide the tracks on the lower level. You may want to make a cliff on one

The buildings usually have their own bases that are large enough for a few people or other details. This layout can be disassembled in less than an hour.

side of mountain. Mountains-in-Minutes offers a choice of three 7x16-inch foam rubber Flexrock textures: 501 Rock Canyon, 502 Rock Embankment, and 503 Rock Gorge, which may be carried or ordered by your Lionel dealer. You can bend the foam rubber rocks in any direction and attach them to the felt with safety pins. The textures and colors are nearly as realistic as real rocks.

A PORTABLE WORLD

The elements of portable scenery are really quite simple. The overall effect is very realistic and better than many examples of plaster scenery because the felt cloth folds naturally into small hills and valleys, and the light on the fibers provides contrasting shades. The lichen bushes add a third dimension, and the trees tie it all together.

Tuck the foam under the edges of the Mountains-in-Miniatures foam-rubber Flexrock and attach the rock cliff to the felt with safety pins.

Lionel's Phantom I fantasy locomotive pulls a train of extruded-aluminum passenger cars through the truss bridge and over the river. This is a portable scene on the 4x7-foot floor layout.

Chapter 9

BUILD A LIGHTWEIGHT TABLETOP LAYOUT

A lightweight tabletop can provide all the advantages of a permanent layout with the added advantage of being portable. There are a number of choices of folding tables, including the Ping-Pong and conference tables described in Chapter 4, but you must remove the track to fold the table. An alternate solution would be a table that is light enough to allow you to leave the track in place and store the completed layout on its side against a wall or slide it beneath a bed.

A BED-SIZE LAYOUT

A 4x6 1/2-foot tabletop will fit nicely beneath a bed and is relatively easy to handle. The track plan is described in Chapter 4 and utilizes 31-inch curves and switches. The small curves and compact size of the layout limits the size of locomotives and the length of the trains.

If you want to operate larger locomotives, consider the alternative 5x9-foot two-level loop-to-loop plan from Chapter 4 that uses 0-72 switches and 42-, 54-, and 72-inch curves. The same construction techniques would be needed for the 5x9-foot version.

A SIMPLE TABLETOP

The simplest tabletop is a sheet of 1/2-inch-thick 4x8 plywood. If you want it to fit under a bed, cut 1 1/2 feet from one end. Most lumberyards will cut the plywood for you.

The ground cover is a sheet of green felt, the trees are freestanding, and the bushes are lichen, so this 4x6 1/2-foot layout is as portable as the cars and locomotives and track. The locomotive is Lionel's 1860s-era 4-4-0 with a combine and coach from the same era.

This 4x6 1/2-foot layout was assembled to match the plan in Chapter 3. There's a station platform, a siding with operating milk car and platform on the lower-level loop; and a station and water tower on the upper-level loop. All of the scenery, including the rock cliffs by the milk car, is portable.

You can make a lighter tabletop with more potential for scenery by using a sandwich of 1/8-inch plywood and 2-inch Dow Corning Styrofoam extruded polystyrene. The white beadboard or expanded polystyrene is too soft for this use. The 1/8-inch plywood must be braced with 1x2 boards along all four edges with a crossbrace across the middle. Use number 8x1 1/2-inch wood screws or drywall screws to attach the plywood to the 1x2s.

Cement a single layer of 2-inch-thick Styrofoam to the plywood, using a common paneling or caulking gun adhesive. The Styrofoam is available in 2x10-foot pieces either 1 or 2 inches thick. The Styrofoam will allow you to cut shallow rivers or streams beneath the track and will help reduce unwanted noises from passing trains.

LIGHTWEIGHT STYROFOAM TABLETOPS

Mark the line you wish to cut with a steel straightedge and pencil. You can cut the Styrofoam with a hack saw blade (adults only, please). The saw produces a lightweight dust that is extremely difficult to control. Have someone assist you and hold a vacuum hose near the cutting edge to capture the dust as soon as it is created. As an alternate, Woodland Scenics makes a hot wire cutter, but it only has about a 9-inch reach. Premium Concepts in Pesto, Pennsylvania, sells the Tippi hot-foam

The 1939-era stamped-steel truss bridge and plastic truss bridge are supported by the upper-level platform (beneath the felt) on one end, and by Lionel plastic bridge piers at the other end of each bridge.

cutter that has a U-shaped blade that can be used like a knife to cut the Styrofoam, but you must cut slowly, and the heated wire will create a crooked edge. The fumes from the melted Styrofoam can be toxic, so always work outdoors and wear a respirator.

In this application, we're avoiding permanent scenery and using the portable felt method described in Chapter 8. With this method, you will need to remove all the track and scenery before you can store this layout on edge, but removable scenery provides the option of changing the track layout whenever you wish.

TWO-LEVEL LAYOUTS

The supports in the Lionel Graduated Trestle set are designed so they can be clipped to Lionel's metal ties, and they can be attached to a plywood tabletop with wood screws. FasTrack trestles can be used in a similar manner. The Styrofoam tabletop is too soft to accept wood screws but the piers are sturdy enough attached to the track, especially so if you clip the track sections together with track clips. I recommend that you clip the joints of a portable tabletop track together with these clips, especially if you are using the graduated trestle supports or

Attach the 1"x2" braces to the 4x6 1/2-foot sheet of 1/8-inch plywood with number 8x1 1/2-inch wood screws or drywall screws.

Opposite, top: The simplest legs are stamped-steel sawhorses. If you want the layout to be higher or the sawhorses support a wider tabletop, buy the sawhorse make brackets and cut 2"x4" wooden legs to the height you wish.

Opposite, bottom: Use a hack-saw blade to cut two 2x8-foot pieces of 2-inch extruded polyurethane foam, like Dow Corning's blue Styrofoam, into 6 1/2-foot lengths and cement them to the plywood tabletop with ChemRex PL300 or Liquid Nails foamboard cement in a caulking gun.

Install the 1x2-inch wood braces around all four edges with a 1x2-inch across the center.

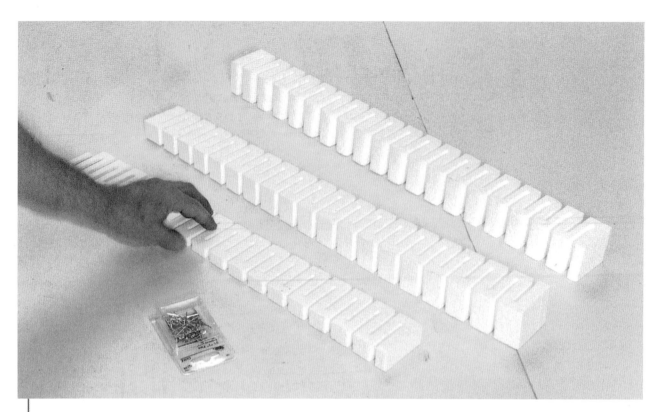

The two tapered Woodland Scenics white polyfoam Inclines (bottom and center) will lift the track from zero to 2 inches above the tabletop. (The Woodland Scenics Riser (top) is 2 inches high for its full length and can be stacked beneath the Risers.) Woodland Scenics also offers T-pins to hold the Risers and Inclines (bottom).

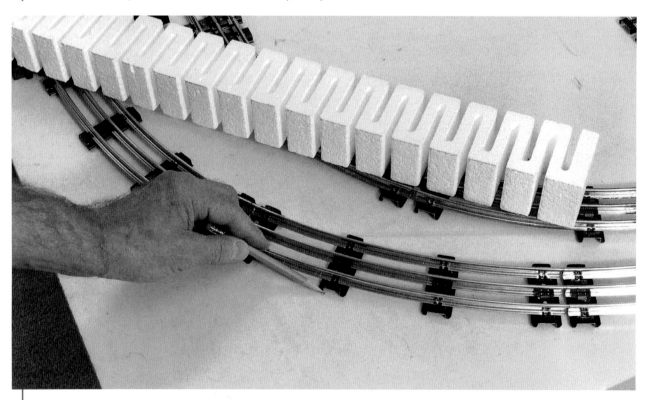

Assemble the complete layout and be sure that every track joint is tight and that the tracks are spaced equidistant from each table edge. Mark the outside edges of the outer curve and straight (the mainline) with a pencil.

the Woodland Scenics. FasTrack ovals can stay together without the need for track clips.

INCLINES FOR A TAPERED LAYOUT

Upgrades for a tabletop layout can be built with Woodland Scenics Styrofoam incline extrusions. These are lightweight white Styrofoam moldings to support the track above the tabletop. The tapered Inclines are molded in a zigzag shape so they can be easily bent to any curve. The steepest Incline is a 4 percent grade, which is 4 inches of climb in 10-inches of length.

Lionel trains must climb about 5 inches if you want one train to pass over another. To raise the track 5 inches with a 4 percent grade, you'll need 120 inches (10 feet)

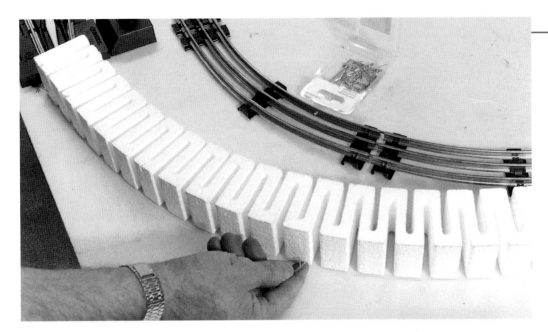

Temporarily remove the mainline tracks to install the Woodland Scenics Risers and Inclines with T-pins. This is the upper end of the grade that will end at 4 inches, so a 2-inch-high Riser is placed directly on the tabletop. The Incline that raises the track from 1 inch to 2 inches will be placed on top of this Riser.

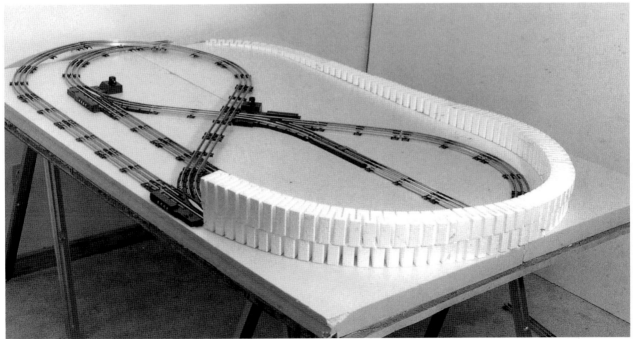

Four two-foot-long lengths of Woodland Scenics Inclines are used to bring the mainline track from tabletop to 4 inches above the tabletop. Note that the last two sections of Inclines are supported by two sections of Risers. The switch at the upper end of the Riser and Incline will be elevated to 4 inches above the tabletop on two 10-inch-long pieces of 2-inch-high Risers beneath the straight section, plus two more 4-inch pieces of 2-inch-high Risers to support the curved section of the switch.

A platform is cut from 1/2-inch board or 1/4-inch-thick plywood to support the upper loop so it can have its own town.

of track. That's about the length of 12 O Gauge track sections. The Woodland Scenics Inclines are 2 feet long, so you will need about 5 Inclines. The Inclines are only available to gain 2 inches of altitude, so you will also need four Woodland Scenics 2-inch Risers. Since the top of the grades is supported by a bridge, we used four Inclines and allowed the ends of the bridge to continue the last inch of the uphill climb.

It is far more realistic to bury the Woodland Scenics track-support system beneath a sheet of felt (for a portable layout) or plaster (for a permanent model railroad). For a permanent layout, you can build an open-grid benchwork without a solid tabletop as shown in Chapter 4.

To install the Inclines on a solid tabletop, mark the edges of the track on the tabletop with a pencil. Remove the track. Install the Inclines and Risers with T-pins, which are sold by shops that sell cloth for dressmaking and upholstery. You can use the same pins to attach the Inclines to the tops of the Risers.

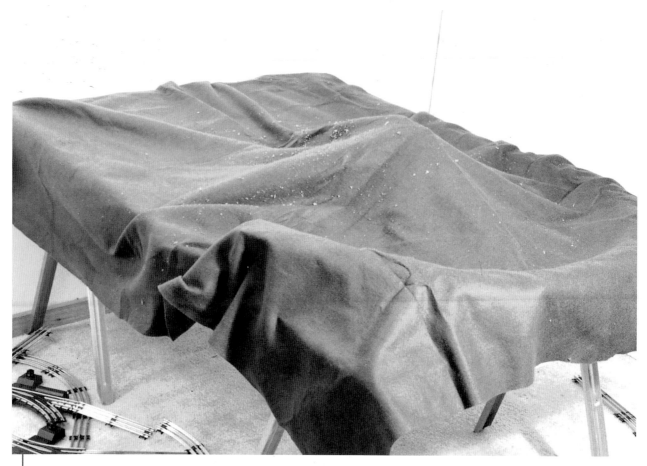

Pile some wadded-up newspaper inside the lower-level loop to create a mountain, then cover the tabletop with a 6x9-foot piece of green felt.

Cut a piece of 1/2-inch foamcore or 1/4-inch plywood to support the upper-level reverse loop. The upper-level board can be supported with bricks (as shown in Chapter 3) or with scraps of 2x6 lumber. You can attach the 2x6s to the bottom of the 1/4-inch plywood with woodworker's cement or to the 1/2-inch foamcore with ChemRex PL300 or Liquid Nail foamboard cement.

PERMANENT-BUT-PORTABLE TABLETOP LAYOUTS

The track, Risers, Inclines, and upper-level supports can be attached permanently to the table with ChemRex PL300 or Liquid Nail foamboard cement. The same cements can also be used to attach the track, applied along each tie or along the FasTrack ballast, to the tabletop. I strongly suggest that you operate your trains for at least a few months and change the track layout and design frequently to try out different track plans, siding locations, and different scenery shapes and structure locations before you make it permanent. Then, when you are satisfied, glue it all in place.

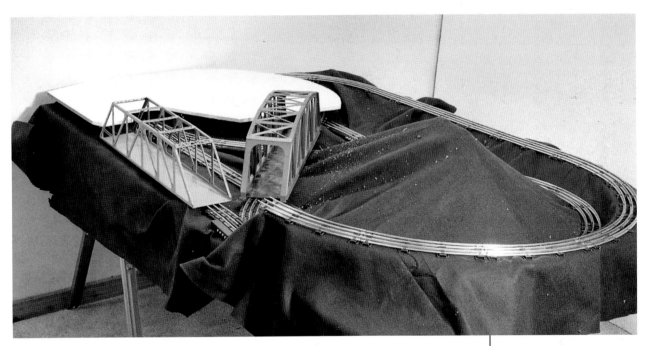

Place the upper-level platform on top of the tracks and mark the inside edge on the felt.

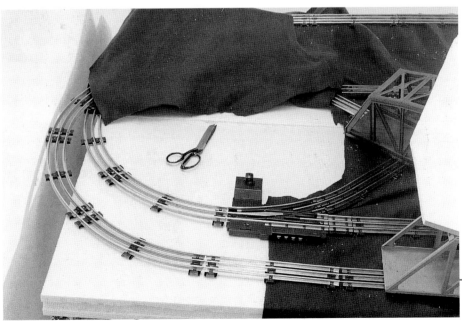

The felt must be trimmed at the edges of the upper-level platform.

The rock faces that separate the upper level from the tabletop level are cut from Mountains-in-Minutes foam-rubber rocks. Use scissors to cut the Mountains-in-Minutes 7x16-inch Flexrock 501 rock canyon to a 5-inch height.

Position the Mountains-in-Minutes 5x16-inch Flexrock around the edges of the upper level platform and tuck the felt around the rocks. You can hold the rocks to the tabletop with T-pins, and use safety pins to hold the felt to the tops of the rocks.

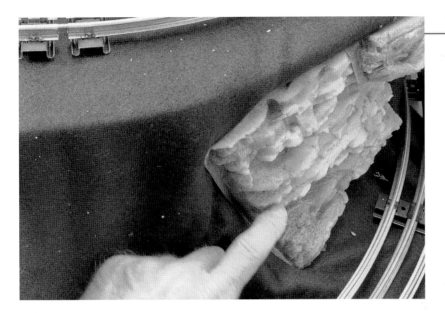

The rock faces are also used to create the sides of a rock tunnel portal on the back corner, with a 1-inch strip of leftover rock pinned to the edge of the upper level platform to form the top of the tunnel portal.

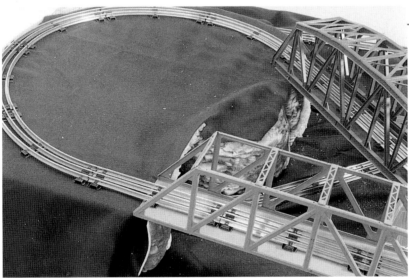

Install the upper-level track and bridges, and smooth out the felt beneath the tracks.

The rock cliff faces are incredibly realistic. The upper ends of both bridges are supported by the 1/2-inch support for the upper level. The lower ends of both bridges are supported by Lionel bridge piers.

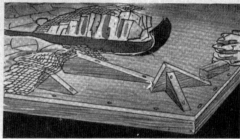

DEMOUNTABLE LAYOUT

THE special feature of this miniature railroad plan is that it can be taken apart in a minimum of time and stored in a minimum of space. In the small drawing immediately above are details of the table construction to illustrate how adequate support might be obtained by the use of only six legs, although more legs might be added to make the layout stronger and sturdier.

In the small drawing at the right, above, is an explanation of the manner in which the hillside is constructed. Blocks of wood are nailed to the table. On top of them, hardware mesh is formed to the contour desired and tacked into place. Then, thin coats of plaster are applied. The track layout shows that there are two lengths of track which must be cut to a special size. Track may be cut by using a hack saw.

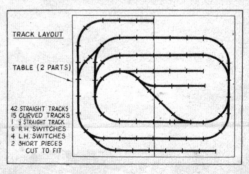

TRACK LAYOUT

TABLE (2 PARTS)

42 STRAIGHT TRACKS
15 CURVED TRACKS
1 ½ STRAIGHT TRACK
6 R.H. SWITCHES
4 L.H. SWITCHES
2 SHORT PIECES
— CUT TO FIT

This Lionel layout is built on a pair of 4x8-foot tabletops with the second table attached to the first to save one pair of table legs. With one exception, all of the track joints are across the joint between the two tables. The hills are shaped with triangles of wood screwed to the tabletop, and covered with a door screen and plaster surfaces. The suggested scenic treatment is simple, with a deep cut in the upper right to keep the height to a minimum if the table is turned sideways against a wall. The only operating accessories are a No. 97 coal loader and a first-generation gantry crane from the 1930s. Four signals are located in appropriate places on the mainline. *Courtesy Lionel LLC, from the March 1943 issue of* Model Builder *magazine*

Chapter 10

PERMANENT SCENERY

Your Lionel trains are as realistic as you could want, but it's up to you to build an equally realistic real-world environment for those trains. Here are some of the easiest to use techniques for creating mountains and canyons, hills and dales, earth and rock textures, and trees and shrub for this book.

THE "ULTIMATE" LIONEL LAYOUT?

It is possible to have both permanent scenery and portable track and structures. Generally, certain parts of the layout table are empty because they are inside loops. Hills and mountains can be placed into those open areas. Valleys, streams, and lakes can be placed just

Mountains-in-Minutes stone walls and tunnel portals are placed between the upper and lower levels on Robert Babas' layout.

Larry LaJambe used broken pieces of 1-inch-thick Styrofoam to shape the scenery and textured it with rough plaster. The bridges are all Lionel and are weathered with diluted black, beige, and brown paints.

about anywhere because you can span them with a wide variety of bridges.

With this portable scenery alternative, you would not use ballast for all-steel O-27 or O track. A good alternative is to switch to FasTrack with built-in ballast or settle for no ballast.

One of the best possible Lionel layouts would be assembled on a table about 8x16 feet or larger that is sturdy enough to walk on, with permanent mountains, lakes, rivers, and FasTrack. The buildings, action accessories, trees, bushes, and track would be completely portable. You have all the realism of scale model railroading with the advantage of changing the track and structures anytime you wish.

CLEARANCE IS CRITICAL

The first rule for building scenery is to make sure the locomotives and longest cars do not sideswipe the mountain, tunnel, action accessory, or structure. Always test run the longest cars or locomotives through any new sections before you attach the scenery permanently to the layout.

A 4-percent grade connects the upper level on Robert Babas' layout with the tabletop level.

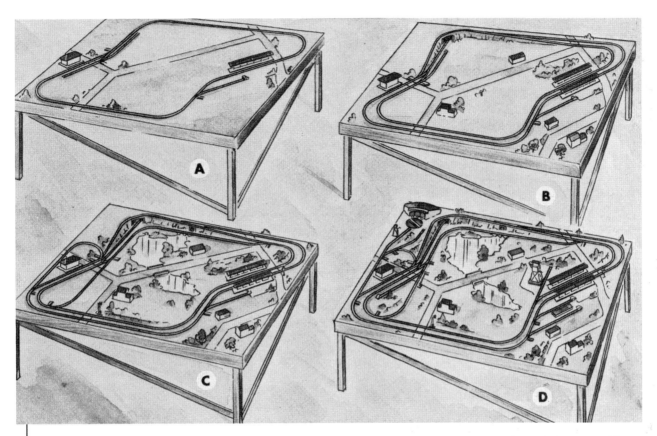

You can start with a 9x9-foot table (two Ping-Pong tables placed side-by-side) and (A) simply cover the surface with felt or ground foam and dirt. (B) Add an up-and-over track along the back wall and a second mainline with some trees and more buildings. (C) You can further improve the layout with another table-level mainline with hills and lakes that are placed inside the loops so the track can be changed if desired, and (D) finish the layout with, perhaps, a roundhouse and turntable and more industrial sidings. *The Model Builder's Handbook, courtesy Lionel LLC*

Lionel track can be attached to a tabletop with a single wood screw though one of the ties in each track section.

If you have a permanent track location, you can apply loose ballast and hold it in place with diluted artist's matte medium.

Shape the hills and valleys with wadded-up newspaper and cover them with Woodland Scenics plaster cloth dipped in water.

Woodland Scenics plaster cloth is impregnated with dry Hydrocal plaster, which can be smoothed and shaped like conventional plaster when wet.

You can also create the scenery with layers of blue Dow Corning Styrofoam. Use a hack-saw blade to cut the hills and valleys.

PERMANENT SCENERY

The traditional method of making scenery for model railroads is to build a wooden framework to support door screening, which is then covered with plaster and textured with sawdust, such as the illustration from 1943. Today, there are much easier and cleaner methods. If you want to use plaster, select one of the plaster-impregnated gauze products like Woodland Scenics plaster cloth. The material is essentially the same as what's used to make plaster casts for broken arms or legs, but it is much less expensive. The plaster is a special product called Hydrocal that sets nearly rock hard. Dry Hydrocal is essentially alabaster. Hydrocal plaster is strong enough to be self-supporting, especially when reinforced with gauze. Since no wire screen is needed, the mountain shapes can be made with simple piles of wads of newspapers.

CARVING STYROFOAM VALLEYS

Builders note: This part of the project should be done by an adult. The alternate method of building scenery utilizes extruded polystyrene insulation board like Dow Corning's Styrofoam. These white insulation boards (sometimes called bead boards) are usually made of expanded polystyrene. Although they are lighter than extruded polystyrene, they are really not strong enough

for rugged scenery. Place at least one layer of 2-inch Styrofoam between the tabletop and the track. Two layers are even better. The thickness allows space for rivers, streams, and roads to be below the level of the tracks.

Carve the Styrofoam with a hack-saw blade or mount the blade in a handle that grips just one end of the blade. The sawing will produce a fine dust that will cling to everything. You can minimize the mess by having a flexible vacuum hose near the cutting area (see Chapter 9) to collect the sawdust as you create it.

You can also carve valleys into the Styrofoam with a heated wire tool like Premium Concepts' Tippi Hot Foam Cutter. The heated wire produces fumes as it cuts through the Styrofoam. Those fumes can be toxic, so always work in a well-ventilated area. The wire can become as hot as an electric stove, and the melted plastic that can drip off the wire is hotter than melted candle wax, so burns are possible. Wear cloth gloves and long sleeves so no skin is exposed. Do not try to use a hot-wire cutter with urethane foam insulation boards, Mountains-in-Minutes, or other poured polyfoam rock, wall or tunnel portal, or styrene castings because the fumes are extremely toxic.

Dow Corning's Styrofoam or expanded polystyrene can be glued with ChemRex PL300 or Liquid

The rock faces on Richard Kughn's layout are chunks of Styrofoam coated with plaster and roughened by hand. The rock faces were painted gray and stained with washes of brown and black watercolors diluted with water.

Nail foamboard cement. Woodland Scenics has a low-temperature foam gun with matching glue sticks that can be used for faster bonds.

To be well prepared, make a 1-inch equal to 1-foot scale model of your layout with child's modeling clay so you can preview the scenery you want to carve. It's far easier to see how steep a slope must be or where a mountain meets the tabletop with clay. You can then duplicate the scenery in Styrofoam or plaster cloth.

CREATING ROCK FACES

Modelers tend to make the slopes of hills, mountains, and the embankments or fills that support the track far too steep. In the real world, a slope that is more than 30 degrees is usually a rock face. If you need slopes that steep, use a rock face. Mountains-in-Minutes offers a choice of three 7x16-inch foam-rubber Flexrock textures: Rock Canyon, Rock Embankment, and Rock Gorge. You can bend the foam rubber rocks in any direction and attach them to the plaster or to the Styrofoam with ChemRex PL300 or Liquid Nail foamboard cement. Your

Lionel dealer can likely provide other choices of precast rock faces, retaining walls, and stone surfaces. These can be placed where you need them before the plaster or Styrofoam mountain is positioned and worked around the rock faces. Protect the rock face with clear plastic while you finish the scenery. You can fill in any gaps between the rock and the hillside with clumps of lichen or wet and wadded plaster cloth.

DIRT AND GRASS TEXTURES

Real dirt is the best thing to use for dirt on your layout, but you must be sure that it has no iron particles that can be attracted to the locomotives' motors and cause short circuits. Test any dirt you want to use with a magnet to be sure that it contains no iron particles. Sift the dirt through a tea strainer to remove the larger particles. Grass and weeds can be simulated by the ground foam rubber that your Lionel dealer can offer from Woodland Scenics.

Cover the surface with undiluted artist's matte medium and sprinkle on the dirt, followed by the

The tunnel portals in this scene on Richard Kughn's layout are Mountains-in-Minutes polyfoam castings. Lionel offers a single-track tunnel portal.

Use a tea strainer to sift real dirt over artist's matte medium to create dirt effects. Sprinkle fine green ground foam to add weed and low brush textures and spray the area with dilute artist's matte medium.

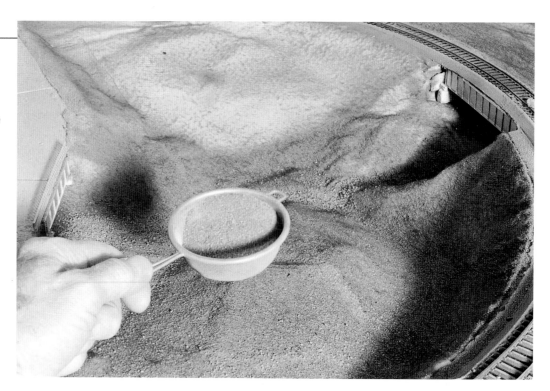

Real dirt and ground foam were used to create the realistic ground cover on the Lionel Visitors Center layout. The trees are made of dried weeds and baby's breath.

ground foam. Work with only about a square foot or so at a time because the matte medium dries quickly. When you are completely satisfied with the surfaces, spray on a mixture of one part artist's matte medium to four parts water plus a drop of two of dishwashing detergent. Completely flood the area so it looks milky white. This final step will minimize the chances that loose texture particles can find their way into the locomotives, cars, switches, and action accessories.

TREES AND BUSHES

Your Lionel dealer can supply a variety of freestanding trees. There are some examples of the larger trees you will want for your Lionel layout in Chapter 8. Pola, Model Power, Life-Like, and Noch offer a variety of 5- to 14-inch deciduous trees and a similar range of coniferous trees. Each tree has large plastic base that simulates the above-ground root structure. The base allows the tree to be free standing. For a permanent layout, you might want to cut off the base and drill a

The vast forests on the Carnegie Science Center and Miniature Railroad Village were created from dried yarrow and dyed queen-of-the-meadow weeds.

There are only nine trees in this scene, but it looks like a larger forest. Life-Like, Noch, Kibri, and Faller make these O scale trees.

hole to accept a 4-inch nail. Push 2 inches of the nail into the hole and leave 2 inches protruding, then cut off the nail head and use the pointed end to push the tree into the plaster or Styrofoam hills and valleys. The nail will allow you to keep the tree vertical and hold it in place. Sprinkle some loose ground foam around the base of the tree and hold it in place with some of the matte medium and water solution.

"REAL" WATER

Clear plastic portable water is the simplest way to create rivers and streams. Most model railroaders prefer to create the stream bed, river, or lake bottom by carving it out of blue Styrofoam or shaping it with plaster cloth.

Small rocks can be used to simulated mountain stream beds. Flood the area that will be the bottom of the water with the mixture of one part artist's matte medium to four parts water plus a drop or two of dish-washing detergent to seal off any air pockets and secure the loose rocks or pebbles. Let it dry for at least a week.

Clear decoupage casting resin, available at craft stores, is a good choice to simulate water. Pour only a thickness of 1/2 inch or less of the decoupage resin into your stream bed or lake bottom and let it cure. Deeper water can be simulated with additional 1/2-inch layers of decoupage resin. Let each layer cure completely before adding the next. You can mix in a drop of dark green food coloring for every 8 ounces of decoupage resin to color the deepest part of the water.

Michael Ulewicz created this small lake with a plaster cloth surface, textured with ground foam. The water is decoupage casting resin with a few drops of dark green and brown food coloring.

The small harbor scene on the Lionel Visitors Center layout has handmade ships floating in decoupage casting resin water.

POPULATING YOUR LAYOUT

Figures do add life to a model railroad. Some Lionel accessories include figures, and the older Lionel plastic building kits included unpainted figures. Lionel also offers a series of painted People Pack figures, including the Lionelville set of neighborhood figures, the station people with six workers and passengers, and the set of carnival people.

Most Lionel figures have plastic bases beneath their shoes to allow them stand on their own. They can also be repositioned from time to time so you can add change and variety to your layout. If you need to customize the figures with your own paint colors, begin with a light flesh tone, and then apply the clothing colors. Finish the figures with a wash of 10 parts water to 1 part dark brown (burnt umber) water color. The dark brown wash will automatically collect in the folds of the cloth, and around eyes, lips, and fingers to provide realistic shadows. If you use too much of the wash, dab it off with a facial tissue before it dries.

You can also add life to your layout with details like telephone poles, billboards, street lights, and vehicles.

An ALCO PA diesel pulls a freight through a Lionel Truss Bridge on the Lionel Visitors Center layout.

This is the all-metal Hell Gate Bridge on the Lionel Visitors Center layout. The bridge was first introduced by Lionel in 1928, and it was recently offered in double-the-track width of the original.

Lionel's 213 Lift Bridge is a massive metal re-creation of a real vertical lift bridge. This is a scene on the Lionel Visitors Center layout.

These vintage figures usually have an unsightly base that can be removed with a razor saw. Heat a straight pin and push it up into the leg so the protruding end can be pushed into the scenery to support the figure.

Some older Lionel kits and accessories have included unpainted figures. To paint the figure, start with the flesh color, then apply the clothing colors, followed by a wash of dark brown to accent the shadows. All new Lionel people packs feature hand-painted pewter figures.

Larry LaJambe's layout is assembled with a 2"x3" wood framework, with a 1/8-inch plywood tabletop covered with a 1-inch layer of blue Dow Corning Styrofoam. The Styrofoam quiets the trains and provides a base in which to carve small rivers and gullies below track level.

Larry LaJambe created this rough sketch of the track locations on his model railroad, primarily to identify different routes for the on-off switches.

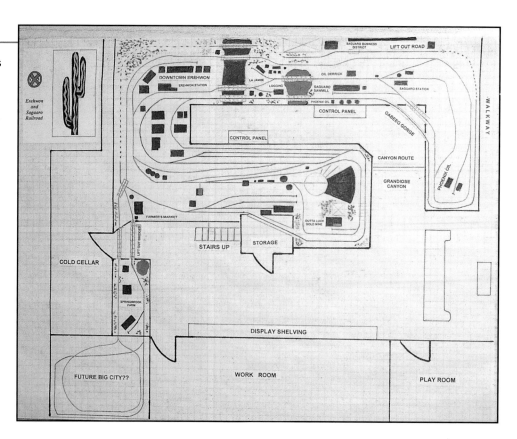

The painted backdrops on Larry LaJambe's layout are made by Walthers. Larry carefully mixed the colors so the scenery would match the backdrops. The cactus and ocotillo plants are carved from balsa wood and painted green.

This panorama is of Michael Ulewicz's Lionel layout. He assembled the track without a plan. The elevated section is reached by an uphill ramp with a 4-percent grade.

This is a panorama of Larry LaJambe's layout. It has a center access and operating aisle that is reached by walking through a tabletop-to-floor canyon.

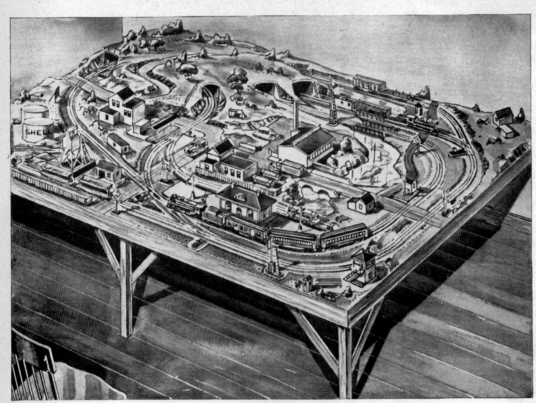

TABLE MODEL RAILROAD

FOR those whose enthusiasm is great, this table model railroad offers a satisfactory solution to the problem of limited space without removing any of the fun of operation by crowding.

Suggesting the use of seven track switches, this particular layout designed by the artist offers a reversing loop and allows for the inclusion of numerous real-life accessories as well as the erection of colorful roadside scenery. The whole layout may be built, if you like, around a complete model town. Also provided for is the possibility of increasing the entire layout size if the builder finds he can obtain additional space later on.

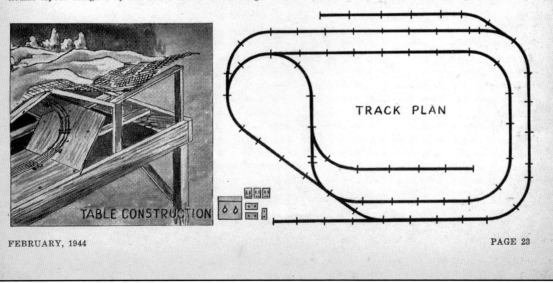

TABLE CONSTRUCTION

TRACK PLAN

This compact layout is about 7x9 feet. The illustration in the lower left reveals the open-grid benchwork of 1x4s with 1x12 supports placed beneath the track (plywood would also work), wood supports for the mountain, door-screen scenery shapes, and plaster mountain surfaces. The scenic treatment icludes signals and a station and station platform, but the No. 97 Coal Loader is the only action accessory. *Courtesy Lionel LLC, from the February 1944 issue of* Model Builder *magazine.*

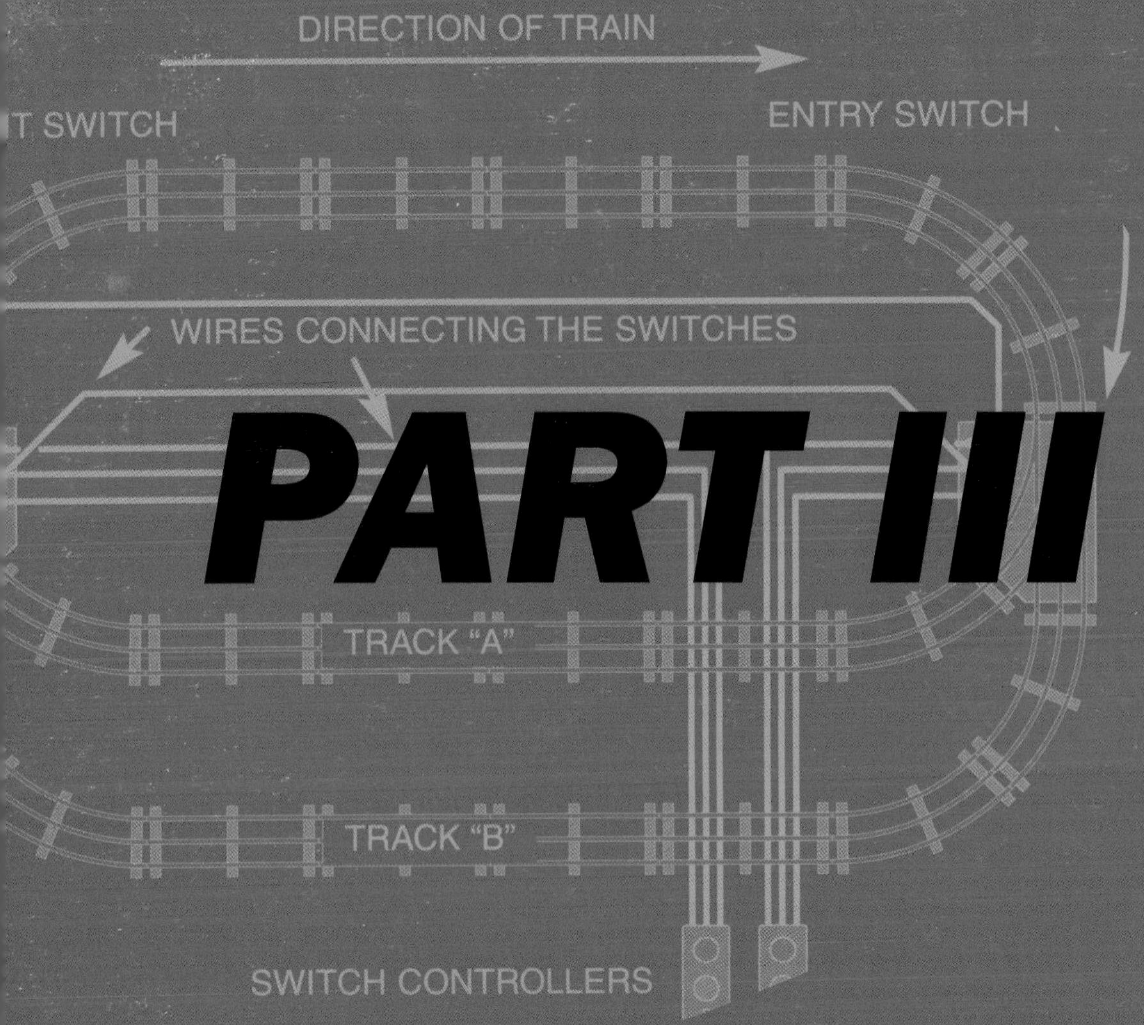

T SWITCH

ENTRY SWITCH

WIRES CONNECTING THE SWITCHES

PART III

TRACK "A"

TRACK "B"

SWITCH CONTROLLERS

Locomotives
and Rolling Stock

Chapter 11

STEAM AND DIESEL LOCOMOTIVES

The romance of railroading centers on locomotives, the massive machines that pull the trains. Today, these 4,000-horsepower diesels are some of the most powerful machines many of us will ever see. On some trains, there may be as many as six of these larger-than-life behemoths. Lionel locomotives effectively capture that mass of machinery in motion. When a Lionel locomotive pulls a train across the floor or tabletop, you can feel the earth vibrate.

STEAM LOCOMOTIVES

The steam locomotive is, to most of us, a symbol of the history and power of real railroading. Steam locomotives are identified by the numbers of the smaller and larger wheels. Pilot wheels are the smaller wheels at the front of some steam locomotives. They guide the locomotive into curves and through switches. The driver wheels are the big wheels that propel the locomotive. The smaller wheels that sometimes follow behind the drivers to support the firebox are called trailing wheels. Steam locomotives, are identified and numbered starting with the pilot wheels, drivers, and then the trailing wheels.

Lionel offers a variety of articulated steam locomotives, including this replica of the Chesapeake and Ohio 2-6-6-2.

The O scale replicas of the Alco FA-2 are super detailed with cab interior.

The streamlined Pennsylvania Railroad 6-4-4-6 articulated is one of the limited-production Lionel O scale steam locomotives.

Most steam locomotives also have identifying names:

2-6-0	Mogul
2-6-2	Prairie
2-8-0	Consolidation
2-8-2	Mikado
2-8-4	Berkshire
4-4-0	American
4-4-2	Atlantic
4-6-0	Ten Wheeler
4-6-2	Pacific
4-8-2	Mountain
4-6-4	Hudson
4-8-4	Northern

Lionel has made them all.

The massive Union Pacific Challenger locomotive has two sets of drivers, with the front set articulated so the locomotive can negotiate tighter curves on the real railroad. The Challenger is a 4-6-6-4 with four pilot wheels, two sets of six driving wheels, and a four-wheeled tailing truck. Both the front and rear sets of drivers are articulated so the model will negotiate the tighter curves.

MINIMUM-DIAMETER CURVES

Many of the larger articulated Lionel locomotives are so long that they will only operate on 0-54 (54-inch diameter) curves or wider, and the largest steamers require 0-72 (72-inch diameter) curves. Lionel offers the LionMaster line, a series of slightly smaller than exact scale steam locomotives, including a Union Pacific Big Boy 4-8-8-4 (the bigger brother of the Challenger). These models are designed to negotiate O Gauge (31-inch diameter) curves.

Generally speaking, if the Lionel steam locomotive model is true O scale, it will require at least a 0-54 or larger curve. These O scale Lionel locomotives are exactly 1/48 scale to match the Standard O series of freight cars. The other Lionel steam locomotives and almost all of the diesels will negotiate the O Gauge curves and switches with no problem. There are track plans in Chapters 4 and 5 that use 0-72 switches rather than O Gauge switches so these larger steam locomotives can be operated on a moderately sized layout.

Lionel produces replicas of the most modern diesels like this O scale EMD SD70MAC.

Lionel has produced a series of O scale replicas of smaller steam locomotives like this Union Pacific 2-8-0 Consolidation.

The Union Pacific 4-6-6-4 Challenger articulated, shown on Robert Babas' layout, is one of the larger Lionel O scale steam locomotives.

DIESEL LOCOMOTIVES

Lionel introduced their first diesel locomotive, a near-scale replica of the Electro-Motive Division (EMD) of General Motors eight-wheeled F-3A, in 1948, just months after the real F3s were delivered.

The real EMD F-3 diesels were offered as an F-3A with a cab and controls and an F-3B with no cab and controlled by the F-3A. The real railroads often coupled these F-3 diesels in sets of F-3A and F-3B, usually called AB or larger four-unit sets of ABBA diesels. Lionel offered the first F-3B back in 1950. Today, new F-3B tools are turning out the newest full-scale superdetailed series of Lionel F-3Bs.

This display in the Lionel Visitors Center illustrates the 12 steps the factory follows to produce a painted F-3A diesel locomotive body shell.

The O Gauge Lionel FA-2 and FB-2 models were introduced in 1948. Although they are much smaller than true O scale, they are popular with Lionel collectors and operators such as Ralph Johnson. The Wabash F-3A, F-3B, and F-3A 3-unit set from 1955–1956 is a collector's item.

The real railroads also operated diesels with narrow hoods, and only the cab was the full width. These were referred to as hood diesels and are the most common diesels on today's real railroads. In 1955, Lionel offered the GP-7, the first in a series of semi-scale replicas of the EMD road switchers that has included replicas of every common railroad diesel.

There are far too many Lionel diesels to list here, but you can be assured that if the locomotive was popular on a real railroad over the past half-century, Lionel has made a replica.

LOCOMOTIVE MAINTENANCE

Fortunately, there is little maintenance with either Lionel steam or diesel locomotives. Lionel's Lubrication/ Maintenance Set includes gear lube, oil in an applicator, track-cleaning fluid, and a track-cleaning eraser.

Clean the diesel wheels or steam drivers every dozen hours or so of operation by scrubbing the direct-to-rail surfaces with the track-cleaning eraser, then wiping the surface clean with track-cleaning fluid applied to

On some Lionel locomotives, like this Phantom III, the adjustments and switches for TrainMaster Command Control and RailSounds are on the bottom of the model.

Clean the areas around the wheels or drivers and the pickup rollers with a pipe cleaner dipped in Lionel Track Cleaning fluid.

Apply a touch of Lionel Lube to exposed gears and a drop of oil to each bearing surface. Use it sparingly. A little goes a long way.

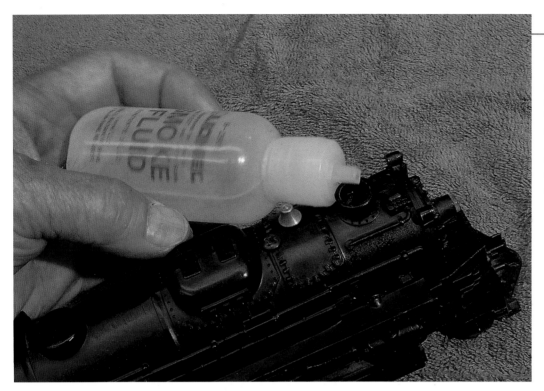

Most Lionel steam locomotives and some diesels have smoke units. Add three or four drops of Lionel Smoke Fluid to produce enough smoke for several trips around most layouts.

This Lionel replica of the General Electric Dash 8-32BWH is a true O scale model with TrainMaster Command Control, RailSounds, Odyssey System automatic speed control, directional lighting, ElectroCouplers, and fan-driven smoke.

a damp rag. Do not ever pour track-cleaning fluid on rubber traction tires. Clean each pickup roller with a rag dampened in track-cleaning fluid.

The gear lube should be used only on visible gear teeth. Use a toothpick to apply a single dab of the lube between each gear tooth, run the locomotive for a few seconds, then use a clean rag to wipe away any excess. Apply one drop of Lionel oil to each bearing. The bearings include each of the pickup rollers and every axle. Freight and passenger cars usually have bearings at the ends of the axles, and diesels and steam locomotives have bearings between the back of the wheels or drivers and the frame. If the ends of the motor's armature shaft are visible, those shafts must also be lubricated with a single drop of oil. Chapter 13 includes methods for cleaning and restoring Lionel locomotives.

DISASSEMBLING LIONEL LOCOMOTIVES

There is seldom any reason to disassemble a Lionel locomotive except to replace a light bulb. In fact, the Lionel locomotives produced during the last few decades are designed to be virtually maintenance free (except for cleaning and adding oil). Lionel recommends that you do *not* remove the body from the newer steam or diesel locomotives, especially those fitted with the Lionel TMCC systems. There are numerous wire connections between the chassis and the body on the TMCC-equipped locomotives, including the antenna, that can be damaged by removing the body, or the wires can be crimped or frayed when the body is reinstalled. Leave any interior maintenance of TMCC-equipped locomotives to your nearest authorized Lionel service station. There are photographs of the interior of one of the SD90MAC Lionel locomotives with TMCC so you can see the control boards, RailSounds board, Power boards, and the R2LC boards. It is like the inside of small computer because, in effect, TrainMaster Command Control and RailSounds are computers.

If you have a train set type of mid-range steam locomotive or diesel, you may want to remove the body to replace a light bulb. On diesels, there are usually just two screws, one at each end of the body. These must be

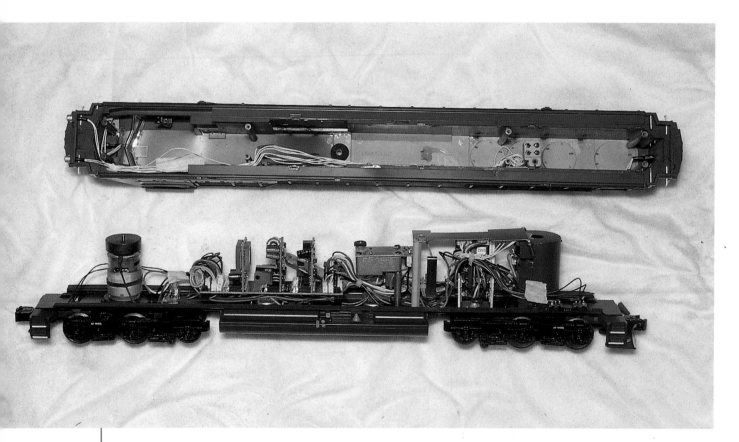

Use great care when removing the superstructure shell from the larger Lionel locomotives, including TrainMaster models, or you may damage the wiring, circuit boards, or antenna. Take the locomotive to your nearest authorized Lionel service station if you are uncomfortable removing the shell. Shell removal is necessary on some engines for battery replacement.

This is the Lionel replica of the SD90MAC that Chuck Sartor at Mizell Trains disassembled as part of his work as an authorized Lionel service-station technician. There is a separate motor with a speed sensor for each truck.

TrainMaster Command Control locomotives also have the Odyssey System speed control and RailSounds. These control boards are for those systems.

The speed sensors are just above the brass rings on each motor, and the electronics for the Odyssey automatic speed control are near the front truck.

unscrewed so the body can be removed. Steam locomotives are always more complicated, but there is usually at least one screw at the front and a pin or second pair of screws at the rear. It's best to bring a steam locomotive into the authorized Lionel service station, even for light bulb replacement.

STEAM SMOKE AND DIESEL EXHAUST
Some of the early Lionel steam locomotives had smoke units that used small pellets to create a smoke effect. All of today's steam locomotives and diesels have smoke units that use Lionel Smoke Fluid to create the effect of diesel exhaust or steam locomotive smoke. Only three or four drops of smoke fluid are enough to create smoke for dozens of feet of operation, so don't try to flood the units by pouring in a lot of fluid. Follow the instructions that come with your locomotive. Even for a trip around a larger layout, a dozen drops are plenty. Resist the temptation to add more fluid until you are absolutely certain the unit has stopped smoking.

Troubleshooting Locomotives

Symptom: Locomotive won't run

1. Be sure all the wheels of the locomotive and all the cars are not derailed.
2. Look at every inch of track for metal objects that have accidentally fallen onto the track.
3. Check to see if the power supply is still plugged into the wall socket.
4. Depress forward/reverse button on the transformer or controller once to be sure the locomotive's reversing unit is not in neutral.
5. Check the connections at the power pack and at the Lockon, and make sure the connections are tight between the transformer and control box if the two are separate components.
6. Try the locomotive on several sections of track to determine if there is a loose track joint or if some parts of the track may be dirty.
7. Try another locomotive to determine if the fault lies in the locomotive or the track and power supply.
8. Remove the two wires from one of the Lockons and touch the bare end of one wire to the third-rail pickup roller on the bottom of the locomotive, and the second bare wire to one of the metal drivers. Turn on the power and see if the locomotive will operate off the track.

This is Lionel's O scale replica of the Chesapeake & Ohio Railroad's 2-6-6-2 articulated.

Chapter 12

FREIGHT AND PASSENGER CARS

The string of freight or passenger cars behind the locomotive is sometimes considered to be the supporting cast. That string of cars is, for many, just a generic train composed of an assortment of shapes and sizes. On a real railroad, freight and passenger cars provide the revenue, and the locomotives provide the romance.

PASSENGER CARS

Real railroad passenger cars were constructed of wood prior to 1900. Steel underframes were later incorporated, and around 1910, cars were made entirely of steel. Lionel has replicas of passenger cars from all these eras.

Lionel offers a replica of just about every freight car that has operated over the past 100-plus years. This is the freight yard on Richard Kughn's Lionel layout.

Since most passenger trains operated day and night, you can run night scenes to show off the interior lighting on the passenger cars with lighted stations and platforms.

An EMD F-7A and F-7B head a Northern Pacific train with a string of four full-vista dome cars and a train of extruded-aluminum smooth-side New York Central passenger cars on Richard Kughn's layout.

Lionel has offered a variety of extruded-aluminum reproductions of real corrugated-steel side passenger cars. These are the No. 9103 Amtrak Vista Dome and the Amtrak Full Dome on the Lionel Visitors Center layout.

Lionel also has three different series of lightweight passenger cars: the short molded-plastic smooth-side streamlined cars that were first introduced in 1948; extruded aluminum cars with corrugated sides that are exact-scale width, but about 10 percent shorter than exact scale; and similar smooth-sided extruded aluminum cars; counterparts to the aluminum cars from the wood-sided era, slightly shorter than the scale length, called "Madison" cars; scale length 18-inch aluminum cars in streamlined and superliner versions; and the older vintage heavyweight cars, similarly equipped and measuring 19 inches long. The newest cars have full-width diaphragms that fill the cab between cars, as well as full interiors with passengers.

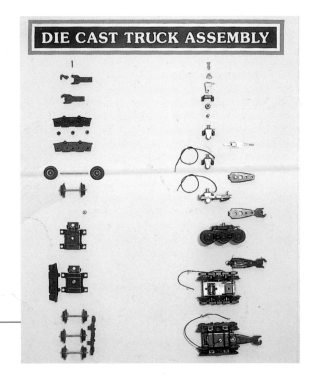

DIE CAST TRUCK ASSEMBLY

The components of a typical Lionel six-wheel diecast truck are shown on this display at the Lionel Visitors Center.

HEAD END CARS

About 40 years ago, real railroads carried most of the country's mail and express shipments in baggage cars, mail cars, combination baggage/mail or baggage coach, express reefers, express boxcars, and milk cars. Lionel offers replicas of all of these head end cars.

FREIGHT CARS

Every freight car on every real railroad was designed specifically to haul a particular type of commodity. All of the different types of prototype freight cars, from the simple boxcar and hopper to unusual cars like depressed-center flatcars and milk tank cars, have been available from Lionel. They are available in a variety of sizes—from compact designs for train sets and smaller layouts, to full-scale versions with a lot of diecast, etched, and wire-formed details.

POP-UP CARS

Some of the more fascinating Lionel cars are the pop-up boxcars and stock cars, in which a figure or animal pops up from a hatch or two on the roof or side. Lionel has offered a variety of pop-up cars over the years, from a series of boxcars that have included an endangered species rhinoceros, a reindeer that pops-up from a hatch on a stock car, a Lionel lion, clown, giraffe, and other figures.

Some of the pop-up cars have two figures, one in each end like the dueling Sheriff and Outlaw Car, Bugs Bunny and Yosemite Sam, Disney's Peter Pan and Captain Hook, and many more.

Lionel pop-up cars have included stock cars with single or double pop-up figures and boxcars like this endangered-species rhinoceros. This Bugs Bunny and Yosemite Sam stock car is on Michael Ulewicz's layout.

The animated gondola has been a popular car for decades. Several variations have appeared, including a sheriff chasing a robber, a lion chasing its trainer, and this Pinkerton detective chasing a hobo.

On Lionel's Bethlehem Steel operating welding car, a brilliant blue light flashes from the welding torch as the car rolls down the track.

Lionel has also offered a variety of short stock cars with windows on one side so animals' heads can bob in and out as the train rolls down the track.

Lionel also offers a series of gondolas with a pair of figures that chase around a load of crates as the train rills down the track. The figures present a chase scene that has ranged from a brakeman chasing a hobo, a sheriff chasing a robber, a lion chasing a lion tamer, Disney's Buzz Lightyear chasing Woody, Cruella DeVil chasing groups of dalmatians, and more.

REMOTE-CONTROLLED OPERATING FREIGHT CARS

Lionel is renowned for bringing real railroad action beyond the movement of the trains over the tracks and through the switches. Lionel offers gondolas and hoppers that carry real coal that can be dumped into trackside bins, and real log cars and flatcars whose logs can be dumped into trackside bins, boxcars that unload crates, milk cars that unload cans of milk, and postal cars that unload bags of mail.

Lionel offers many variations on the Postwar log and coal dump cars and the more realistic Lionel Lines log and coal dump cars. The Lionel Operating Hopper Car (with operating hopper doors on the bottom) can dump coal into a bin between the rails like real railroad hoppers. The Lionel Operating Coal Ramp is designed to be used with Operating Hopper Car.

Lionel has offered a variety of remote-control log-dump cars including (left to right) a series of Lionel Lines log-dump cars with a simple magnet and mechanical release, a smaller all-steel 361 lumber car from the late 1930s, and the longer classic log dump car from the 1930s that Lionel has reintroduced in plastic and metal for a number of years.

The Lionel Operating Gantry Crane has an electromagnet that can be used to load and unload steel rails and ties from gondolas, like this scene on the Lionel Visitors Center layout.

Lionel operating accessories are designed to be loaded and unloaded by Lionel Action cars. The metal No. 97 Electric Coaling Station, No. 397 Coal Loader, and Log Loader are arranged on a pair of sidings on Richard Kughn's layout.

Lionel has also offered cattle cars that load and unload cattle and other animals. Lionel's Operating Horse Car and Corral has been available as a Circus Car with white horses, an Animated Reindeer Stock Car and Corral with brown reindeer, and several versions of a cattle car with cows, including a yellow CNW car.

Conventional gondolas (or any Lionel Coal Dump cars) can also be loaded with steel rails, ties, or spare steel track clips and dumped in the bin to be reloaded by the Magnetic Gantry Crane.

LIONEL'S OPERATING MILK CAR

The true classic of all Lionel operating cars is the Milk Car, in which a worker pushes cans of milk out the door onto a waiting platform each time you push the remote-control button. There have been many variations of the car since its introduction in 1947, but the action has been the same for nearly 50 years.

Current Lionel Milk Cars have a steel ramp that guides the milk cans into the waiting arms of the milkman. A wire-wound solenoid is activated by the electronic circuit that is completed when the car is parked over the remote-control track. Push the remote-control button on the remote-control track and the milkman pushes the doors open to deposit a can of milk on the steel platform supplied with the Operating Milk Car.

Lionel Operating Boxcars that feature a mail carrier who pushes mail bags out the door, or similar cars that have a small figure pushing crates or barrels out the door, operate on a principle similar to the Lionel Operating Milk Car, except these cars have a simpler mechanism that can be actuated by the electromagnet in the Lionel uncoupling track or similar magnets in the remote-control tracks.

ACTIVATING THE ACTION CARS

Most Lionel operating action freight cars are activated by stopping the car over the O-27 uncoupling or remote-control tracks, the O Gauge remote-control track, or the FasTrack uncoupling track and pressing the remote-control operating button. These track sections will actuate any Lionel cars with a 1/2-inch diameter flat pin on the bottom of the car. They will also activate automatic couplers with that pin. Some Lionel equipment from the 1940s and 1950s, and some of the modern cars, including the Operating Milk Car, are fitted with small rectangular pickup shoes to activate the unloading feature and couplers. These cars are activated with remote-control tracks.

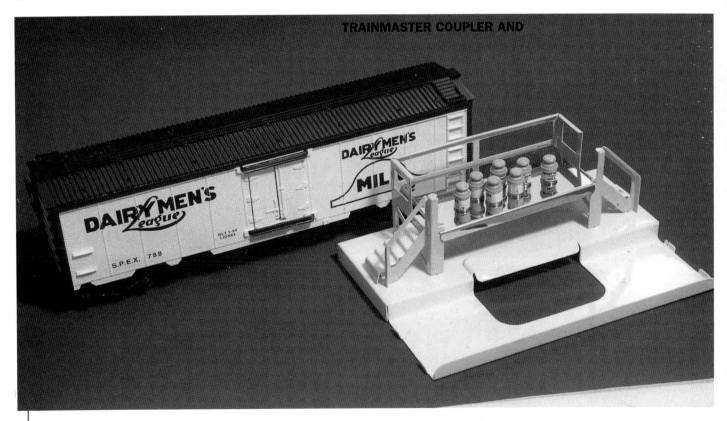

This Dairymen's League is typical of Lionel's newer series of operating milk cars. The metal milk platform and the milk cans come with the car.

ACTION CAR CONTROL

The remote uncoupling tracks or remote-control tracks can be activated by pushing a button on the TrainMaster CAB-1 Remote Controller. You will need to install an Operating Track Controller (OTC) to do this. Each OTC will operate two remote-control track sections or four uncoupling track sections. The TMCC CAB-1 can also be used to operate ElectroCoupler-equipped cars or locomotives anywhere on the track.

TROUBLESHOOTING ACTION CARS

When a Lionel Log Dump or Coal Dump Car, Operating Milk Car, or Operating Boxcar fails to function, the fault almost always lies in a jammed mechanism. Log and Coal Dump Cars sometimes have bent lock-down levers that can prevent the load platform from pivoting upward. Check the mechanical operation of these cars by holding them stationary on the track by securing one of the trucks with your hand and pulling down on the shiny metal disc that sits beneath the chassis to determine if the mechanism is functioning smoothly. Clean any debris or oil from the mechanism and hinge pins with a pipe cleaner dipped in Lionel track-cleaning fluid. A drop of oil on the hinged ends and latch will sometimes improve the operation.

The best way to avoid jamming any Lionel action car is to be sure that it is completely unloaded when you put in back in the box.

If the Operating Milk Car fails to operate, first go through the troubleshooting steps in this chapter. You will likely discover that one of the milk cans is jammed

To disassemble the operating milk car, remove the screw from each end of the car.

inside the car. Remove the body from the chassis by removing the screws from the ends of the car that hold the cover plate on the milk chute. Any jammed cans should be visible. Try operating it with the bare chassis over the Remote-Control Track to see if the mechanism is operating properly, and if so, reassemble the car.

If a particular car derails, it may be because it is one of the lighter pieces of rolling stock pulling heavier cars behind it. Sometimes, when operating really long trains, it's best to put the lighter cars near the rear of the train. If lighter cars consistently derail, you might want to replace the plastic trucks with diecast metal trucks, or to fill them with cargo to add weight and stability.

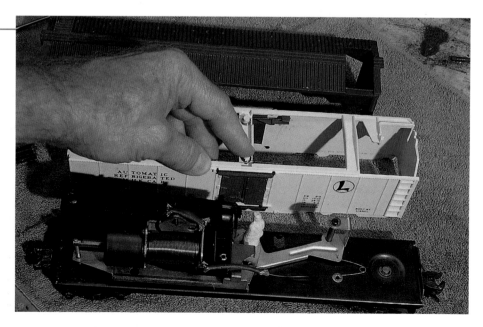

The operating milk car has three major pieces: roof and ends, sides and body, and frame. The doors are held shut with hairpin springs.

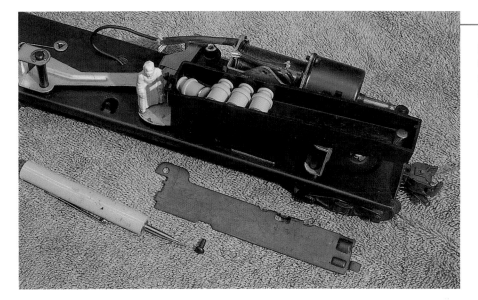

Remove the screws that hold the cover plate over the milk chute. You can then remove any jammed milk cans from the chute.

Troubleshooting Freight and Passenger Cars

Symptom: Car derails
1. See if only one car derails. If more than one car derails at the same point, the fault is likely a loose track joint.
2. Check for accumulated dirt or gum on one or more wheels. Clean the wheels thoroughly.
3. The truck may not swivel properly due to grime or foreign matter at pivot point. Clean the pivot point and, if necessary, pry the truck gently away from the underframe with a screwdriver until the truck is free to swivel from side to side.

Symptom: Remote-controlled couplers won't couple
1. Both knuckles (one on each of the cars) must be open for the cars to couple properly.
2. Couplers will not couple on a sharp curve. There should be at least one length of straight track on each side of the remote control or uncoupling track
3. The coupler mechanism may be jammed. If wiggling the pin up and down does not free it, try a drop of oil. If that fails, take the car to an authorized Lionel service station.

Symptom: Remote-controlled couplers won't uncouple.
1. One of the uncoupling discs must be centered directly over the round magnet in the center of the remote control or uncoupling track. Move the car back 1/2 inch and try the remote-control button, then move the car forward 1/2 inch.
2. Try several cars. If none uncouple, the wires from the remote control or uncoupling track to the button may be loose where they connect to the track or are wired in the wrong sequence.
3. The coupler knuckle may be jammed. Try operating the coupler by pushing down on the lever on the side or by pulling down on the magnet, then opening the coupler by hand. If the coupler is sticky, a single drop of oil might be enough to allow it to operate freely.

Chapter 13

PAINTING AND RESTORING LIONEL MODELS

L ionel locomotives and cars have an exquisite style. Their colors and crisp markings make the models even more appealing. Lionel has either offered or is likely to offer just about any paint scheme you can dream of, and you can usually find the paint scheme you want if you are willing to search for used equipment or wait for future releases.

It is possible to restore older equipment without ruining the paint scheme. And, you may not be willing to wait for Lionel to paint and letter a locomotive or car to match your favorite railroad, especially if it's a local short line road. The painting and restoration techniques developed over decades by HO and O scale model railroaders will work equally well with Lionel equipment.

CLEANING LIONEL CARS AND LOCOMOTIVES

If you operate your Lionel trains, they are eventually going to get dirty. The good news is that they can be cleaned. In fact, even some of the oldest and grubbiest garage sale finds can be restored.

Older used Lionel equipment can be pretty filthy, with an accumulation of dust and grit held firmly with a dried, caked film of oil. You cannot wash a locomotive or car in the dishwasher, but you can use mild liquid detergents to dissolve the grime. I don't recommend any type of abrasive powdered cleaners or coarse scrubbing pad. Patience and a stiff fiber-bristle brush will be enough to remove everything except the paint. You can reach into the smaller areas with a cotton swab or a pipe cleaner dipped in detergent. If the grime is truly stubborn, you can try denatured alcohol, but it can often dissolve the paint and lettering, so test it on an inconspicuous spot before you remove more than the dirt.

The Burlington Northern locomotive is a Lionel GP-9 that began life with a CNW paint scheme. The red caboose can also be painted to match other railroads.

These passenger cars are examples of 607 Pullmans and 608 observation cars from the mid-1920s. The cars will be worth less if they are repainted, but they are definitely worth cleaning and restoring.

Lionel produced these cabooses by the thousands, so there are plenty of inexpensive used ones available in the aftermarket, at swap meets or online auction sites.

Use detergent and an old toothbrush to remove grime. Use caution around lettering and decals.

A cotton swab dipped in alcohol may be needed to remove some stains. Work in a well-ventilated area and wear a respirator when working with alcohol or paint.

Hobby shops carry a variety of model railroad paint you can use to touch up chipped areas. Floquil Boxcar Red was a good match for the brown on this caboose.

When the model is completely clean, rinse it thoroughly, dry what you can with a soft rag, and finish the job with a hair dryer. Do not, under any circumstances, hold a locomotive, car, action accessory, or action car under running water. Use a wet rag to remove any leftover detergent.

RESTORING LIONEL CARS AND LOCOMOTIVES

If the cleaning process produces a model that is acceptable, leave it. If there are rust spots, they should be removed with a liquid rust remover and rinsed thoroughly. You can try to match the paint to cover the rust spots or leave the metal bare. Train Enamel, from Charles C. Wood & Co., is available in several colors matched to older Lionel equipment. You can restore the shine by spraying the model with several light coats of clear gloss, which will protect the bare metal and paint. Cover any clear plastic windows with masking tape, because the clear gloss often produces an etched or crazed effect on clear plastic.

There are Lionel-approved expert restorers who can repaint and reletter a Lionel car, locomotive, or accessory so it looks as good as new. They usually charge about as much as you would pay to buy a good original, so the choice is yours. If you have an heirloom that you want to repaint, and you understand that it will be less valuable to collectors when you are done, give it a try. I couldn't find any decals to replace the Lionel Lines or the Lionel logo. You could reletter the Lionel Lines a

letter at a time using the alphabet sets that Microscale offers. If, however, you really want it to look new, leave it to an expert.

REPAINTING LIONEL CARS AND LOCOMOTIVES

Model railroaders in other scales paint and letter their cars and locomotives as an integral part of the hobby. There are several choices of paints and decals to enable you to create an accurate paint scheme for most full-size railroads. Model railroad paints are matched to color chips from the real railroads and have a flat finish. All can be applied with an airbrush, a miniature version of the spray guns used to paint real automobiles. Your hobby dealer can order airbrushes and air supply systems. Floquil and Scalecoat also offer most colors in aerosol cans. Testors Model Master series of paints (available in jars or aerosol cans) are intended for military modelers, but many of the colors are useful for railroad modelers, especially for painting structures.

I restored an older Lionel caboose, then decided what I really wanted was that same caboose in Union Pacific colors. Lionel has offered a similar car, but it didn't have the exact paint and lettering scheme that I wanted, so I repainted mine. I used an aerosol can of Scalecoat Union Pacific Armour Yellow to paint the car, then masked the sides of the body and cupola and sprayed Scalecoat Boxcar Red on the roof. The decals are Champ CN-105, which were intended for a stock car, but they were what I had on hand.

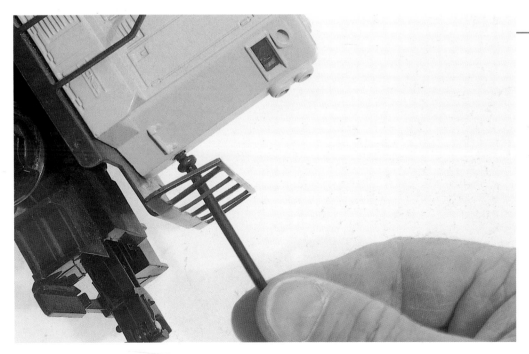

It is easier to repaint a model if you can remove the body. On some less expensive O 27 diesels, the body is attached with a screw in each end.

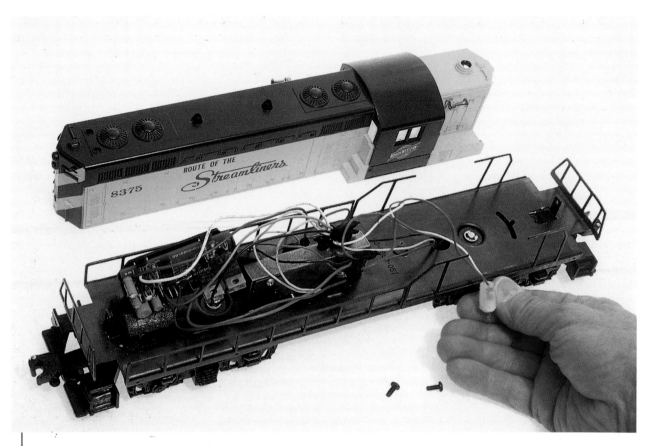

The light bulb inside this diesel locomotive clips into a bracket in the roof. Remove the light bracket and gently remove the windows, marker lights, and headlight lenses before painting.

Bend a wire coat hanger to make a handle to hold the model while spraying. Tape the ends of the hanger inside the model.

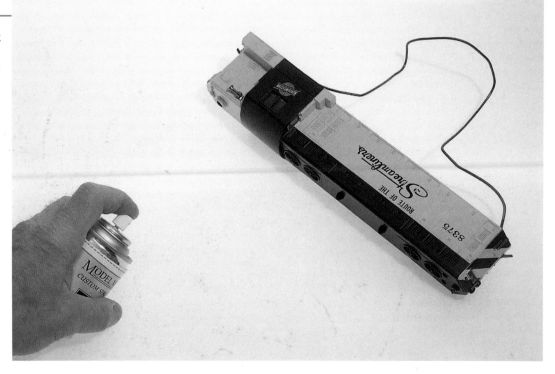

Clean the model thoroughly before painting. Unless you are starting with a bare metal model, primer shouldn't be necessary. If you are using two colors, start with the lighter color. It's best to remove the body from the chassis and remove any clear windows and lights before painting so you can avoid masking them. Bend an old coat hanger to use as a handle and tape the ends of the hanger inside the model

Spray paint flows best when used at 70 degrees or higher, and you need to work in a well-ventilated area. I try to work in the backyard on a warm and windless day. Always wear a respirator when working with paint. Wear disposable rubber gloves to protect your hands. Hold the model about a foot from the spray can and start the spray away from the model, sweeping the spray pattern over the model and off the other side before releasing the button. It is best to apply about three or four light coats, and let each coat dry for at least four hours so there is no chance of the paint accumulating and running or sagging. You may need more coats if you are trying to cover a darker color with a lighter color.

The C&NW GP-9 in the photos is a 1989 model that Lionel introduced as an entry-level locomotive in a set. About a decade later, Lionel offered a similar C&NW GP-9, with a different road number, as a TMCC special. Only two screws hold the body to the 1989 engine. I do not recommend that you remove the body from the later GP-9 or from any Lionel model with TMCC because there is too great a risk that you will damage the TMCC receiver, RailSounds, and other electronics. If you want to repaint a locomotive equipped with TMCC, have your nearest authorized Lionel service station disassemble the model and reassemble the repainted body.

PAINTING TWO COLORS

To paint a two-color scheme, apply the lightest coat first and let it dry for at least a day. If the color separation lines are straight, use Scotch Magic tape to cover the first color. The Magic tape allows you to see if the tape is actually stuck tight because the loose areas are cloudy. If the color separation areas are curved, you can cover the area with Magic tape, use a hobby knife (adults only, please) to slice the tape along the curved lines, and then remove the excess tape. Protect the rest of the model with conventional masking tape.

Spray on the second color, starting with two light coats to seal the masking, then use as many coats as needed to cover the model properly and let it dry for 24 hours. Use a hobby knife to slice along the edge of the now-painted Magic tape to cut the paint from the edges of the tape. Gently peel off the tape, pulling the tape back over itself rather than straight up to minimize the chances of lifting the first color. You may find that there are a few areas that need to be touched up to make a perfect color separation line. Spray some of the paint in the lid of the spray can and use a number 0 paint brush to touch up any fuzzy areas.

For a two-color paint scheme, spray the lighter paint color first and let it dry, then mask off the lighter color with Scotch Magic tape along the edges. Use plain masking tape to cover the rest of the body. When you remove the tape, peel it back over itself, as shown.

To remove the caboose body, gently pry the metal retaining tabs upward on each end platform.

You can wiggle the body free without bending the retaining tabs all the way. If you only bend the tabs part way up, they will be less likely to break.

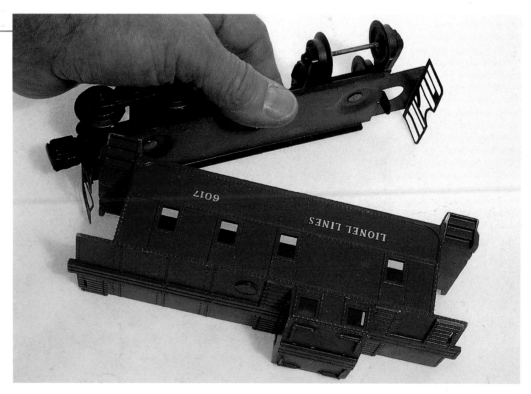

On this caboose, I left the roof brown and masked it off to paint the sides and ends on the body and cupola. For painting a complex area, you can use Microscale's Micro Mask masking fluid.

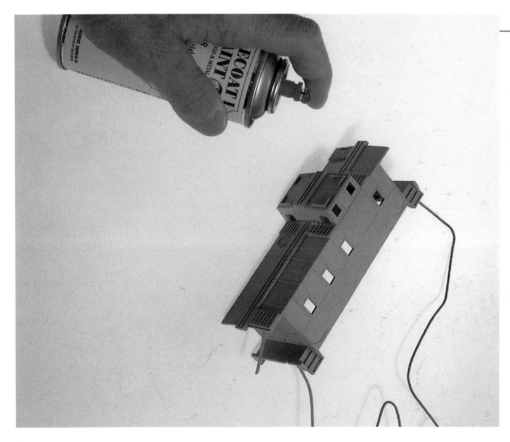

Apply the Microscale Micro Mask masking fluid to cover the brown areas, then apply the second color. I used Scalecoat's Union Pacific Armour Yellow.

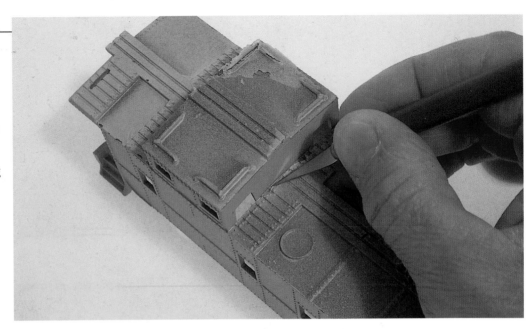

To remove the Microscale Micro Mask, slice along all of the edges between the masking fluid and the yellow. Pick at one corner with a hobby knife until you can grip the dried masking fluid with tweezers.

Gently pull back the dried masking fluid with the tweezers.

If the model you are painting has a complex color separation line, like the roof on a caboose, you may want to use a masking fluid like Microscale's Micro Mask. Apply the lighter paint color first and let it dry. Brush on the Micro Mask fluid and cover about 1/8-inch more than you actually want to mask. Let the fluid dry overnight. Use a sharp hobby knife to slice through dried Micro Mask along the color separation line. Then gently peel off the excess Micro Mask. Spray on the second color and let it dry. Again, slice through the paint along the color separation line. The Micro Mask can

now be peeled away. Start by picking at one corner with a sharp hobby knife until you get a large enough piece to grip with tweezers. Finally, use a number 0 paint brush to touch up any ragged edges or places you forgot to mask.

LETTERING LIONEL MODELS
Your dealer can order Microscale, Champ, and Walthers O scale model railroad decals. The Champ and Walthers decals have the clear area over the entire sheet so you must cut as close as possible to the letters or heralds

You will probably need to touch up some of the color separation edges with a No. 0 brush lightly dipped in paint.

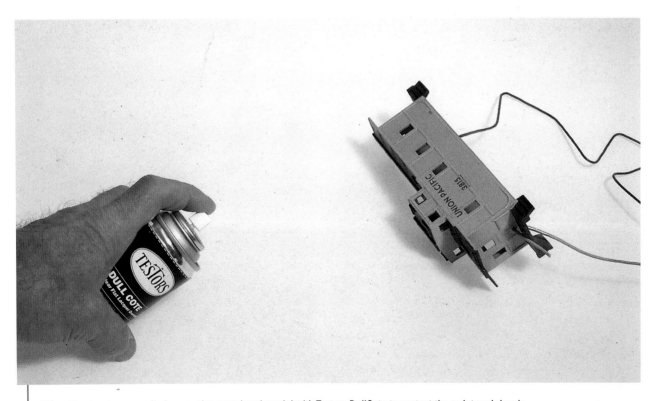

When the decals are applied, spray the completed model with Testors DullCote to protect the paint and decals.

The repainted caboose is a custom model you'll only find on one Lionel layout in the world.

when removing the decals from the sheet. Microscale covers only the lettering or herald portion of the decal with clear area, so it is a bit easier to cut the decals apart.

To apply decals, first cut each decal from the sheet. Dip only decals you are going to use on one side of the car into warm water using tweezers. Just submerge the decal, then immediately place it on a facial tissue for about a minute so the water has time to soak through the paper backing to dissolve the glue on the back of the decal. Put a drop or two of water on the area where you will be placing the decal. If the area has a complex shape, like the curve of diesel nose or the panels, hinges, and latches on the side of diesel body, apply a coat of decal-softening fluid like Microscale Microsol before you position the decal. Lift the decal and paper backing with tweezers and position them on the car. Slide the decal about 1/16 inch off the paper backing with the tip of a hobby knife. Grip the exposed paper

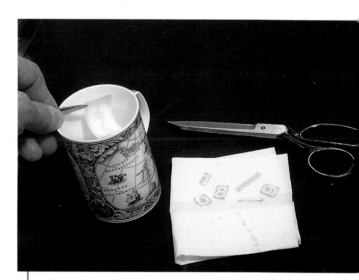

Cut each decal from the sheet, and get as close to the letters and numbers as you can. Dip the decal in water and rest it on a facial tissue while the water soaks through the paper backing.

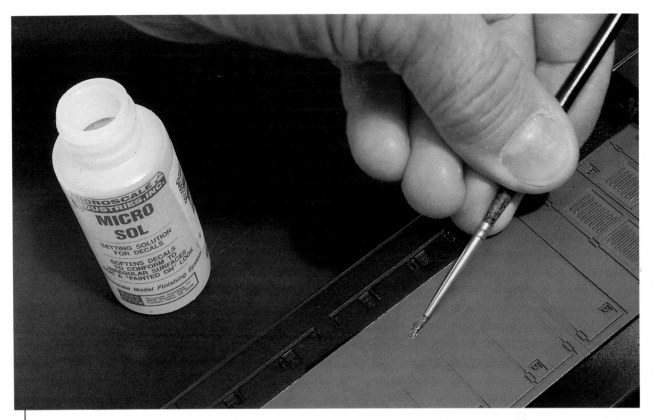

If the decal is going to be applied over a complex area like the hinges and panel seams of a diesel body, apply a coat of Microscale Microsol right before you position the decal.

Position the decal and the paper backing, then pull the paper backing from beneath the decal and slide the decal into the proper position with the tip of the tweezers.

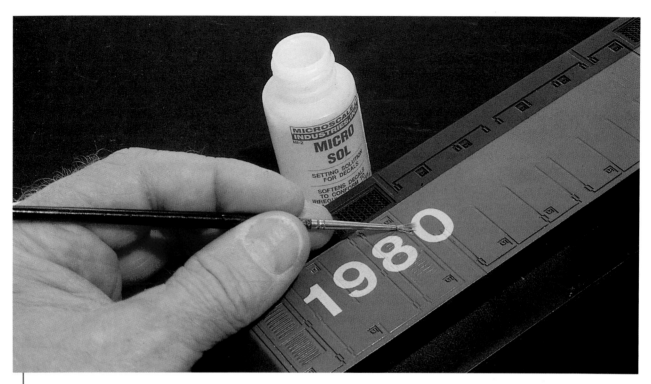

Apply a second coat of Microscale Microsol to the top of the decal and let it dry completely.

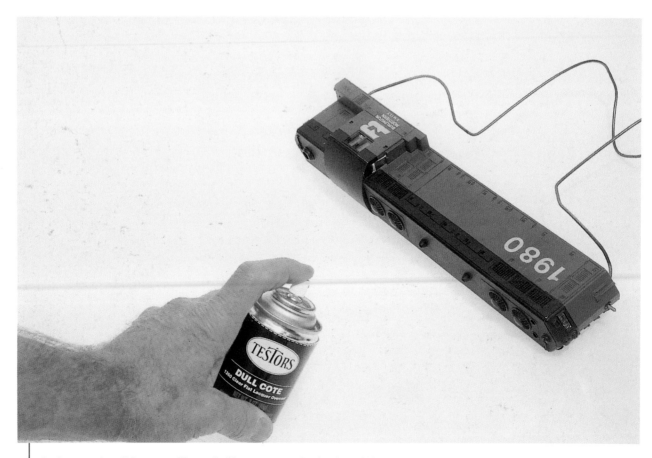

Apply two or three light coats of Testors DullCote to protect the decals and blend them into the overall color of the model.

Install the clear windows, number boards, and headlight lenses, and secure them with a drop of white glue or Testors clear parts cement.

The body is ready to be reinstalled on the chassis.

backing with tweezers while you hold the decal onto the model with a number 1 size paint brush. Position the decal exactly where you want it and wick away any excess water or decal-softening fluid with the corner of a facial tissue. Paint over the decal with a single coat of Testors Model Master decal setting solution, Microscale Microsol, or Walthers Solvaset decal softener. These fluids literally turn the decal into soft paint so it will adhere more tightly to the surfaces and flow into the seams and around rivets.

Do not touch the decal for 24 hours. The decal should fit as tightly as the paint. On some really deep seams, you may need to use a sharp hobby knife to slice along the decal. Turn the model over and repeat the entire application process for the lettering on the other side and for each end of the car. Gently scrub away any dried

When you install the body, make sure that all the wires are tucked inside so none of them are pinched between the body and the running boards or other parts of the chassis.

softener residue with a damp tissue or cotton swab and let the model dry for a few hours. Finally, spray the model with Testors DullCote to provide an even luster to the decal and model and to protect the decals. If you want a slightly glossier finish, use Testors Model Master Semi-Gloss clear.

You will derive a special satisfaction from creating your own unique piece of rolling stock or customized locomotive. You'll know that there is only one in the world, and it's on your Lionel model railroad.

There is an alternative to decorate your train without decals. It uses similar, but slightly less durable art materials called rubdowns. For many years when Lionel introduced new products and put them in the new catalog or take them to conventions, the prototypes would be painted and decorated with rubdowns.

The process of applying rubdowns is very easy. Once you've placed a piece of art in the proper position, secure it with tape or hold it in place. Lightly, but firmly, rub the glossy transfer sheet to transfer to decal to the surface of the train car.

Rubdowns, like decals, can be tricky. You must make sure you position the decal in the exact spot you want because any shift in placement during the application process could cause the art to crack, which would show on the finished product. When it is finished, the rubdowns can look so much like a manufactured finished product that an untrained eye can be fooled.

J&A Hobbies, in Waynesboro, Pennsylvania, is an official Lionel rubdown provider. Their phone number is (717) 762-4424.

The finished Burlington Northern diesel matches this Lionel extended-vision BN caboose.

PART IV

Operating a Real Railroad

Chapter 14

OPERATE LIKE A REAL RAILROAD

Lionel trains are operated by individuals, just as real railroad locomotives are. The engineer has the responsibility of starting and stopping the train, slowing for curves, and keeping the train on the tracks. You are the engineer of your Lionel locomotive.

REMOTE-CONTROL UNCOUPLING
You can recreate the essential real railroad operations of delivering one carload at a time on your Lionel layout without touching the car.

All Lionel train sets have cars that can be remotely coupled. With remote-control coupling and uncoupling, you have the buttons of the uncoupling or remote-control track, or if you are using TMCC, the button on the CAB-1 to control your operations.

Lionel cars and locomotives are equipped with one of three different styles of automatic couplers. Each of the three has the opening-knuckle action of a real railroad coupler.

The most common Lionel couplers are actuated mechanically by a pin similar to those on real railroad

The passenger trains on your Lionel layout can recreate the express trains that only stopped at major stations like this standard gauge passenger station with lighted station platforms on the Lionel Visitors Center layout.

couplers. There is a round plated-steel tab smaller than the size of a dime suspended from the bottom of this tab below the coupler. When the coupler and tab are positioned directly over the center of a Lionel uncoupling track or remote-control track, they activate a small electromagnet in the center of these track sections with its remote-control button. When the magnet is activated, it attracts the small disc on the bottom of the coupler to pull the pin and open the coupler. There is also a small black tab protruding from the side of some of the couplers that can be pressed to manually uncouple the couplers.

Some older Lionel cars and locomotives are equipped with an electromagnet coupler with the operation coil mounted inside the truck. These couplers are activated by power that is picked up by the small rectangular pickup shoes on the trucks. When they make contact with the fourth and fifth rails of the special remote-control track sections. The fourth and fifth rails are then energized by the push of a control button.

The third type of Lionel coupler is the Electro-Coupler fitted to most TMCC-equipped locomotives and cars. The ElectroCoupler also has its own electromagnet, but it can be actuated anywhere on the track by simply pressing a button on the handheld CAB-1 remote controller.

Lionel offers a choice of three special tracks to actuate these couplers, the O-27 remote-control track, the O Gauge remote-control track, and the FasTrack uncoupling track. These track sections can also be used to activate the remote-controlled freight cars that unload or provide other animations, as shown in Chapter 15.

Cars and locomotives will not couple or uncouple reliably if there is a curved track on either side of the uncoupling or remote-control track. To be sure the couplers will always operate properly, plan to have at least one full length of straight track connected to both ends of the uncoupling or remote-control track.

YARD SWITCHING

On a real railroad, the yard is the place where trains from one city are broken down into trains heading to two or more cities. Trains are assembled from individual cars by a switching locomotive.

In this oversimplified example, the railroad yard would have five sorting tracks, an arrival track (where a train from Chicago is parked at the moment), and a

You can couple or uncouple cars by lifting one car about 1/2 inch above the other to engage or disengage the couplers.

Most of the automatic couplers on Lionel cars and locomotives have a small black lever beside the coupler that can be pressed to open the coupler knuckle.

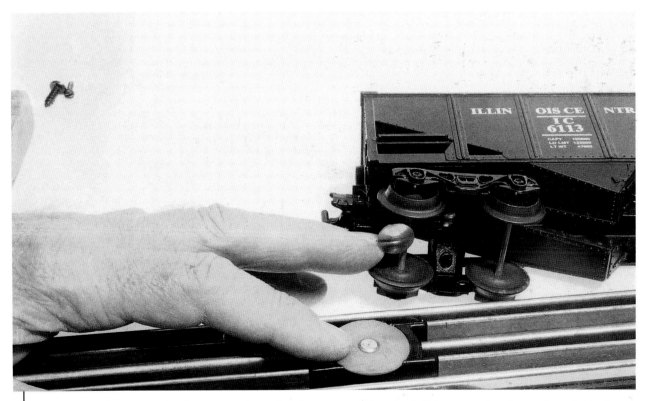

Most Lionel cars and locomotives have automatic couplers that are actuated mechanically by a magnet on the remote control track or uncoupling track that attracts the bright metal disc or rectangular steel plate on the bottom of the coupler arm to open the coupler knuckle.

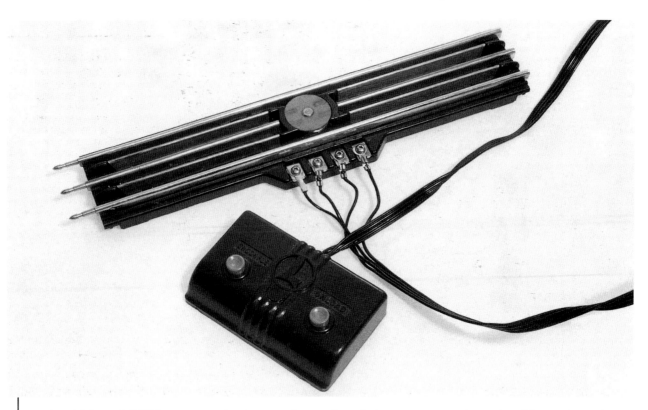

The Lionel O Gauge 6-65530 remote-control track uses track power. Press the button to open couplers and send the cars into action.

Some of the older Lionel cars (and now some of the newest ones)and locomotives have electromagnetic couplers that are actuated by this small rectangle pickup shoe that provides contact with the fourth or fifth rails on the remote-control track.

The TrainMaster locomotives and some larger freight cars are fitted with Lionel's ElectroCouplers that can be uncoupled anywhere on the track using the TrainMaster Command Control system.

Denver, Austin, San Francisco, and Seattle track. The road locomotive(s) would uncouple from the train so the yard's switch engine could break down the train to put the cars routed to Denver on the Denver track, the cars routed to Austin on the Austin track, and so on. Later in the day, additional trains would arrive from Chicago with more cars routed to customers in these four cities, and, once again, the switch engine would break down the train and sort the cars onto the tracks for their eventual destinations. When there are enough cars for a full train to Denver, a road engine would be called up from the engine terminal, and the locomotive and caboose would be coupled onto the train so it could head to Denver.

TRAIN CONTROL BY SIGNALS

Real railroads have dozens, sometimes hundreds, of trains on the same track at the same time. To keep these

A Santa Fe Super Chief streamliner rumbles away from the station platforms on Michael Ulewicz's Lionel layout.

Lionel offers dozens of operating accessories that duplicate
real railroad customers who receive and ship freight cars,
including this operating freight station.

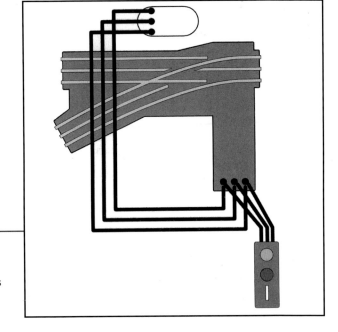

If a block signal or a semaphore is wired to the switch as shown at
right, it will indicate green "go ahead" when the switch is set for the
train to move along the main line, and red "stop" when the switch is
set for the train to turn into a siding. The operating Gateman can
also be operated in this way.

A modern and a Postwar pair of Lionel magnetic cranes serves this scrap yard on Richard Kughn's layout.

trains from running into one another, a series of signals, much like the traffic signals you see on the street, is used. Signals have been part the Lionel line for a century, and replicas of most common real railroad signals are available. The diagrams illustrate the type of signals used during the first half of the past century. Today, the signals are usually two or three lights, or there may be signals in the cab of the locomotive. For a model railroad, the glamour of early era signals is exciting to duplicate.

SIMPLE SIGNALS, MORE MAGIC FROM THE THIRD RAIL

If you want the appearance of real railroad signals, you can connect the signals' three wires to the control box on the nearest switch. The signal will turn from green to red (or the semaphore arm will drop from vertical to horizontal) when the switch is turned from the mainline to the branchline. You can swap the end wires to have the signal indicate "stop" for either route.

Lionel's 153C contactor switch can also be used so the train itself actuates the signal. The 153C is operated by the weight of the locomotive, which closes an circuit switch to change the signal.

I recommend for applications like this that you consider using the Lionel insulated track sections for O-27, O, and FasTrack as described in Chapter 6. The insulated track sections can be substituted for the 153C with minor changes in the wiring. The insulated track section

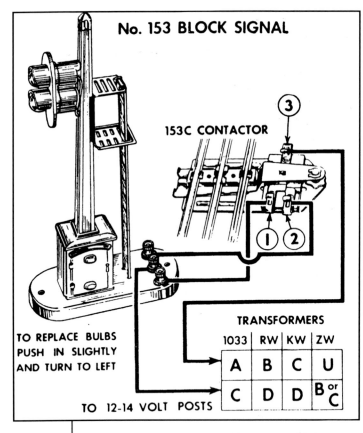

No. 153 BLOCK SIGNAL

153C CONTACTOR

TO REPLACE BULBS
PUSH IN SLIGHTLY
AND TURN TO LEFT

TO 12-14 VOLT POSTS

TRANSFORMERS

1033	RW	KW	ZW
A	B	C	U
C	D	D	B or C

Each signal can be wired to a 153C contactor, 153 IR contactor, or insulated track section for automatic control. *Courtesy Lionel LLC*

merely provides an electrically isolated outer rail that is used as an electrical trigger, actuated by any locomotive or car, to operate signals or warning devices. Because both outer rails receive power, the insulated rail is a simple method to provide automatic control that is only possible with a three-rail track system like Lionel's.

An alternate method would be to use the Lionel 153IR controller that looks like a trackside maintenance shed. The 153IR controller's simulated shed houses an infrared light source and detector. The 1531R can be adjusted for time delay from 0 to 20 seconds so you can time the amount of warning an approaching train receives from the signal.

TRAINMASTER COMMAND CONTROL SIGNALS

One feature that TMCC does not offer is protection from collisions. In fact, that is one of the best features of the system. You have to assume the complete responsibilities of a real locomotive engineer, including being on the lookout for signals and/or other trains. Lionel offers a variety of signals, and there are simple signal-actuating devices to allow the signals to function much like those on a real railroad.

TMCC can be used to actuate signals so you have the choice of using the TMCC system or Lionel traditional contactor devices or insulated track sections as described in Chapter 6.

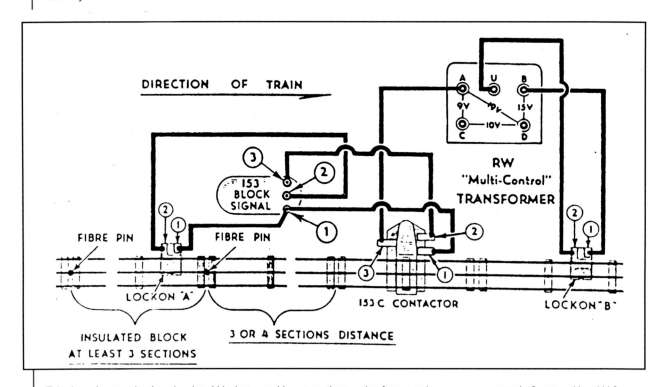

This shows how to wire three insulated blocks to provide automatic stopping for two trains on a one-way track. *Courtesy Lionel LLC*

SIGNALS FOR TWO OR MORE TRAINS

Chapter 7 explains how to wire a Lionel model railroad so you can run two or more trains, each with its own electrically insulated block. You can use the 153C contactor to actuate any of the automatic block signals or automatic semaphore signals. Each signal can be connected to a Lionel 153C contactor. An insulated track section can be substituted for the 153C contactor, as described in Chapter 6.

If you want a series of signals on a one-way track to be actuated by two trains, a train-length block (3 or 4 track sections) of insulted track must be placed before the signal to provide a place for the train to stop if the signal is red. The diagram shows how to wire the 153C contactor to the block and Lockon in the insulated block just to the left of the stopping block. Each of the three blocks (the one at the far left, the stopping block, and the block with the Lockon) is isolated from the rest with the fiber pins in the center rail. FasTrack offers an equally easy option using its Accessory Activator Pack.

If you are using the TMCC system, the blocks can be controlled from the CAB-1 by wiring the blocks to a Block Power Controller (BPC) or you can use conventional on-off switches, as shown in Chapter 7. The signals can be actuated with the TMCC Accessory Switch Controller (ASC) or SC-2 Switch Controller.

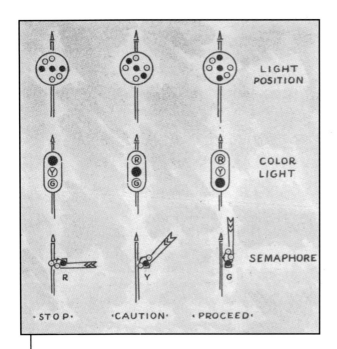

These are three common styles of real railroad signals. The dark spots are the illuminated lights. *From* The Model Builder's Handbook, *courtesy Lionel LLC*

SIGNAL SETUP FOR OPERATION

Real railroads locate signals at specific locations. The most obvious locations are on single-track mainlines to keep opposing trains from having head-on collisions. The railroad's dispatcher uses the railroad's timetable to try to schedule trains so they meet at passing sidings and not on the mainline. On a real railroad, there are often dozens of miles of single- or double-track mainline without a siding. Sometimes these long stretches of track are broken into signaling blocks so a faster train can slow down behind a slower train until the slower train reaches the next passing siding.

The other obvious locations are junctions at other railroads. A model railroad is not usually large enough to have two independent railroads, but 45- and 90-degree crossings are often part of a Lionel layout. These crossings will look far more realistic if two operating signals are installed near them.

The drawings illustrate the usual places where real railroads position signals. The signals in the drawing are all semaphores, but the locations would be the same for either banjo or block target signals. Drawings A and B show the right and wrong positions for a signal on a blind curve. Drawings C and D show the locations of signals at either end of a one-way railroad's passing siding or where a branchline railroad leaves or joins the mainline. If the railroad is two-way, like drawing E, the signals would be located at the entrance or exit of the branchline and mainline.

A two-railroad crossing with both of the railroads having one-way traffic is shown in drawing F. If both railroads are two-way, four signals should be needed, facing the opposite directions from the two shown.

Drawing G shows a complete signaling system for a large model railroad, including a three-track gantry to trains leaving and departing a passenger or freight terminal. Drawing H indicates where signals would be positioned on a more compact layout. On layouts G and H, the block signals are located near the positions where the electrically isolated blocks begin and end, as described for two-train operation in Chapter 7. The blocks are at least the length of one train, with an insulated fiber pin in place of the steel pin in the center rail at both ends of the block to electrically isolate that section of track. A switch allows the power in that block to be turned on or off. An alternate method that doesn't require blocks is to use the TMCC system.

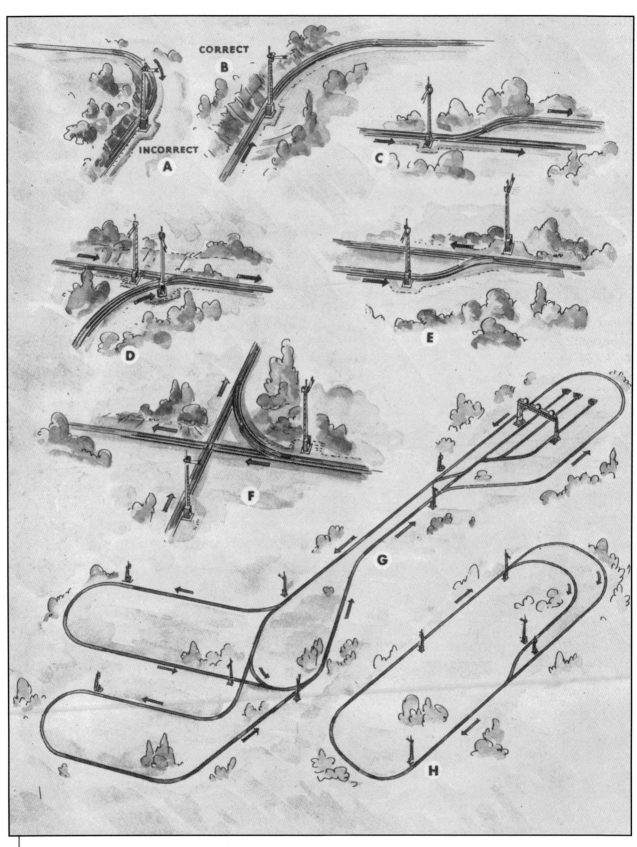

These are the correct positions for signals with specific real railroad track arrangements and how they could be used on two Lionel layouts. *From* The Model Builder's Handbook, *courtesy Lionel LLC*

RIGHTING WRECKS

Real railroads have derailments, just like those on your Lionel layout. Real railroads do not, however, have a giant pair of hands to right the cars and locomotives and place them back on the track. Lionel offers a variety of wrecking cranes, including the manually operated Derrick cars, self-propelled Burro cranes, 12-wheeled Bucyrus Erie cranes, or the completely remote-controlled massive 12-wheeled TrainMaster Command Control crane car. You can make a rule that any derailments have to be rerailed using the hooks and cables on the Lionel crane car. It will certainly take a lot longer than just picking the derailed cars up by hand, but it's a lot of fun to recreate the real railroad's wrecking crew operations. For added realism and easy operation, you may want to have two TMCC crane cars.

Lionel also offers a series of maintenance an inspection vehicles so you can simulate real railroad functions and help prevent wrecks. You can send one of the variety of Lionel self-propelled railroad speeders, handcars, on-track pickup trucks, gang cars, fire cars, or you can send one of the self-propelled Lionel rotary snowplows around the track to be sure that no snow has accumulated to block the trains.

A self-propelled Lionel Burro Crane works to rerail a wrecked caboose at the site of a grade crossing accident.

Lionel Burro Cranes have been available in a number of railroad liveries, including this Union Pacific model with matching gondola.

Lionel has offered many variations of self-propelled railroad maintenance vehicles including the Burro Crane, railroad speeders, handcars, gang cars, rotary snowplows, fire cars, and this on-track pickup truck.

Chapter 15

MOVING FREIGHT

Real railroads provide the empty cars, but it's the loads packed inside those cars that provide the income to keep the railroads in business. Lionel offers a wide range of freight cars that will actually accept a load from one of the Lionel action accessories like the log or coal loaders, cars that unload like the operating milk car, and a series of action boxcars.

Builders note: Be sure to check a current Lionel catalog or consult with your local Lionel dealer on the availability of products mentioned throughout this book. Product lines change from year to year, and

In the early 1990s, Lionel offered a simple plastic snap-together kit to build a manually-operated barrel loader like the one in front of the No. 464R operating sawmill on Michael Ulewicz's layout.

some items may not always be offered on a consistent basis.

REAL LOADS FOR MORE REALISTIC ACTION

Any Lionel open-top flatcar or gondola or operating log and coal car can be loaded using Lionel operating accessories like the Log Loader or Conveyor Log Loader (you can also dump the logs into the sawmill or use the American Flyer Log Loader to load the log-dump cars). The American Flyer Sawmill simulates a log being cut into timbers and uses a boom and cable to load the timbers into waiting gondolas. Specially equipped gondolas can also have culvert pipe sections loaded and unloaded by remote control using the complex 345 Culvert Unloaded and 342 Culvert Loader.

In the past, Lionel offered a simple plastic snap-together kit to build a manually operated log loading station and a similar kit to build a manually operated barrel loader. This kit is a little hard to find today.

The coal-unloading cars can be loaded, remotely, with the No. 397 Coal Loader Conveyor, or with the chain-belt-buckets of the metal No. 97 Electric Coaling Station, the elevated hopper of the No. 497 Coaling Station, or the clamshell and tower of the metal No. 752 American Flyer Seaboard Coaler. The modern unit-train bathtub coal gondolas can be unloaded using the massive Rotary Coal Tipple (using coal specifically designed for this accessory) or the No. 456R Operating Coal Ramp with No. 3456 Operating Hopper Car.

Lionel also offers the No. 362 Operating Barrel Loader that recycles barrels. The barrels are dumped in the receiving bin and moved up a conveyor to reload them into a standard gondola or the Operating Barrel Car.

Four action accessories are featured in this industrial park on Richard Kughn's layout, including three coal-loading accessories. The red and green structure in the foreground is the No. 497 coaling station, the beige structure with a red roof is the No. 97 coaling station with chain-belt-buckets to hoist the coal into the tower, and the angled gray conveyor of the No. 397 coal loader is just visible behind it. The green, yellow, and red accessory is the log loader.

The No. 464R operating sawmill on Michael Ulewicz's layout has a spinning saw blade that appears to slice through the massive logs.

Lionel's No. 362 operating barrel loader moves barrels from the receiving bin up a conveyor and into either a standard gondola or the operating barrel car that can dump the barrels back into the bin to repeat the cycle.

The American Flyer oil drum loader has a small forklift that shoves the barrels of the platform into an awaiting gondola.

The 345 culvert unloader and 342 culvert loader form a remote-controlled, hands-off industry that can automatically load or unload one culvert at a time into a waiting gondola. Lionel has also offered several variations of the barrel loader that roll barrels into special gondolas.

Most Lionel action cars have a small steel disc on the bottom that is attracted when the electromagnet in the operating track section is energized. The steel disc pulls down to release the load of coal or logs or activate the worker that throws bags of mail, barrels, or crates out the door of a boxcar.

THE LIONEL ICING STATION

Lionel's Icing Station is one of the more popular action accessories, and its operation very exciting to watch and activate.

The Icing Station is a Lionel accessory that has had a long and useful life. It was introduced in 1955–1957 as the No. 352 Ice Depot, then reintroduced as No. 6-2306 in 1982. These earlier icing stations looked almost identical to the modern version, but the operation of the earlier station was actuated by a solenoid with a plunger. The Icing Station, introduced in 1988–1989, and the more modern 6-14158 icing stations are powered by a motor with a lever attached to the shaft that moves the iceman as he pushes each block of ice into the open hatch in the roof of the special Lionel Ice Car.

Lionel has offered a variety of ice cars. The blocks of clear plastic ice are loaded into a hatch in the roof of the car. Inside the car, the blocks are moved down a chute to be unloaded through the door in the side of the ice car.

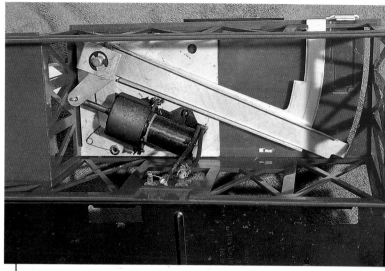

Lionel ice depots, produced from 1955 to 1957 and reintroduced in 1982, were activated by a solenoid with a plunger to operate a lever that moves the worker pushing ice into waiting ice cars.

The worker on the Lionel icing station automatically pushes blocks of clear plastic ice into the open rooftop hatch of one of the Lionel ice cars on Michael Ulewicz's layout.

The icing stations that were produced since 1988 have an electric motor that motivates the worker on the platform to push ice into the waiting ice cars.

Robert Babas built a pair of rails from old track sections to guide the wheels on the legs of his magnetic Gantry Crane.

The Southern Pacific Intermodal Crane on the Lionel Visitors Center layout moves forward and back, and the container rack grips and lifts the containers and moves them right to left.

PICK 'EM UP AND PUT 'EM DOWN

Two of the most fascinating accessories in Lionelville are the Gantry Crane that has either a hook or a working electromagnet to pick up steel, and the intermodal crane that grabs, hoists, and carries intermodal containers. Both of these accessories are operated by control boxes with levers to allow you total remote control.

THE WAYBILL OPERATING SYSTEM

Many model railroaders find that operating freight trains is far more enjoyable and more realistic if each and every car is designated as loaded or empty and has an appropriate destination.

Real railroads prepare a waybill for every carload shipment. The shipper, receiver, and shipment are all listed on the waybill. Modelers create smaller replicas of the waybills on 3x5-inch cards. I suggest making three or four waybills for each car.

For our purposes, a small clear plastic packet the size of the index card is used to simulate the waybill board on a real railroad car. A self-adhesive label on one corner of the card gives the type and number of the car, and that envelope stays near the car. You may want to provide a few small boxes to hold the car envelopes and loose waybills near some of the towns or yards where you might spot or pick up freight cars.

The cycle for each standard type of waybill and the plastic envelope for each car is shown in the diagram. Notice how the car (with its matching clear plastic envelope car packet) can begin the operating sequence wherever it is on the layout. The operating cycle can begin in the yard, which might be wherever the train was parked the last time it operated. The waybill is first inserted into the car packet. When the car arrives at its destination, the waybill is turned over and placed back in the envelope unless the car is unloaded at that industry. The waybills for unloaded cars go back to the yard and the empty car travels with an empty envelope.

To create the waybills, make photocopies of the four waybills here. If you have more than a couple of dozen freight cars, you might want to use different colored cards for different types of cars so the waybills are color-coded by car type. Cut each of the four sections apart on the cut lines. Fold each of the four sections over, back to back. Cement the plain backs together with rubber cement to create a waybill card.

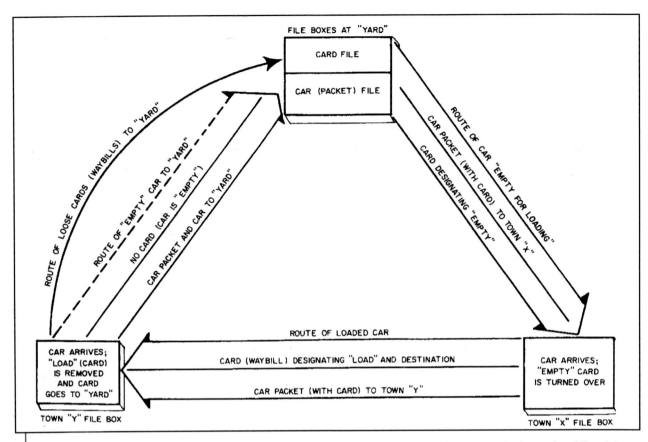

FILE BOXES AT "YARD"

CARD FILE

CAR (PACKET) FILE

ROUTE OF LOOSE CARDS (WAYBILLS) TO "YARD"

ROUTE OF "EMPTY" CAR TO "YARD"

NO CARD (CAR IS "EMPTY")

CAR PACKET AND CAR TO "YARD"

ROUTE OF CAR "EMPTY FOR LOADING"

CAR PACKET (WITH CARD) TO TOWN "X"

CARD DESIGNATING "EMPTY"

ROUTE OF LOADED CAR

CARD (WAYBILL) DESIGNATING "LOAD" AND DESTINATION

CAR PACKET (WITH CARD) TO TOWN "Y"

CAR ARRIVES; "LOAD" (CARD) IS REMOVED AND CARD GOES TO "YARD"

TOWN "Y" FILE BOX

CAR ARRIVES; "EMPTY" CARD IS TURNED OVER

TOWN "X" FILE BOX

The waybill operating system provides a simulated load for every freight car. This is the cycle for each standard type of waybill and the plastic envelope for each car.

The components of the waybill operating system are (left to right): colored waybills (not yet cut apart, folded, or cemented), clear plastic pocket protectors (to hold a train of waybills), 3x5-inch clear envelopes to hold the colored waybills, 3/4x1/2-inch white stickers, an empty business card box, and file dividers you can mark with the car types.

CUT → FOLD ON DASHED LINE

CUT

When delivery is made, separate card from packet. Place empty packet in "Town" set-out box. Place card in "Yard" file.

When delivery is *made*, turn over waybill and file waybill and packet in "Town" set-out box.

CUT

CUT

When delivery is made, separate card from packet. Place empty packet in "Town" set-out box. Place card in "Yard" file.

When delivery is *made*, turn over waybill and file waybill and packet in "Town" set-out box.

CUT

When delivery is made, separate card from packet. Place empty packet in "Town" set-out box. Place card in "Yard" file.

When delivery is *made*, turn over waybill and file waybill and packet in "Town" set-out box.

CUT

When delivery is made, separate card from packet. Place empty packet in "Town" set-out box. Place card in "Yard" file.

When delivery is *made*, turn over waybill and file waybill and packet in "Town" set-out box.

CUT

Photocopy this page. You can choose different colored paper for different types of cars.

Cut each of the four sections apart, fold each over, and cement the backs together with rubber cement (from a stationery store) to produce the waybills for the operating system.

Buy enough matching 2 1/4x3 1/2-inch clear plastic envelopes to match the number of freight cars you have (or hope to purchase in the next year or so). Finally, buy an equal number (or more) of 1/2x3/4-inch self-adhesive labels to identify each clear plastic envelope. You can color code them with felt-tipped pens, if you wish. Empty business card boxes may be available at some printing companies and make nice boxes to hold the cards and plastic envelopes.

SETTING UP THE WAYBILL SYSTEM

With this waybill system, you only need to do the paperwork once. Start with a list of all the cars you own or intend to buy in the next year. Write down every imaginable commodity that might be shipped in each of those cars.

Make a separate list of all your industries. An industry can be an empty siding where you plan on placing a new action accessory or Lionelville building. Any siding, even if it only has one piece of straight track, can serve more than one industry.

Try to think of some industries that receive, and other industries that ship. Try to locate both the shipping and receiving industries on your layout. A Lionel Log Loader might be paired with a Lionel No. 464R Operating Sawmill or an American Flyer Sawmill. Be sure that you have listed all the commodities each industry might either ship or receive. Write the word "in" in blue beside each commodity the industry might receive, and the word "out" in red beside each commodity each industry on your list might ship.

The interchange yard is where the railroad exchanges cars with its competitors. Designate one part of the a siding as an interchange yard. You might designate it as AT&SF Westbound Interchange or Conrail Eastbound Interchange. Cars can remain in the interchange yard overnight (how ever many days or minutes you feel is enough) before being considered empty and ready to return to the yard or shipping customer. Extra cars can be stored on shelves beside the layout. Also, remember to set up sets of loads for the recycling action accessories like the log and coal loaders.

Here are a few examples of how you can list industries and commodities that those industry ship or receive:

INDUSTRY	COMMODITY	CAR TYPE
Creamery	Milk cans in	Milk car or reefer
	Empty milk cans out	Milk car or reefer
	Milk cans out	Milk car or reefer
	Empty milk cans in	Milk car or reefer
Grain elevator	Grain out	Covered hopper
Sawmill	Rough logs in	Log car
	Smooth logs out	Log car
Logging camp	Empty cars in	Log car
	Rough logs out	Log car
Coal mine	Coal out	Hopper
Coal dealer	Coal in	Hopper
Coal-Grader	Coal in	Hopper
	Coal out	Hopper

Enter the car type to identify the car and match each car to the commodity for the load it is supposed to carry on the waybills.

Make a second list of all the industries you have created for your model railroad. Make two more columns beside each industry, one marked "to" and the second column marked "from."

List the imaginary city and industry that would ship the commodity to your industry under the "to" column. These are the places where the carloads are going to be shipped to your industry.

List the industry that would receive the commodity shipped by your industry under the "from" column. You can add the city, if you wish.

The operations will be more interesting if at least three-fourths of both the "from" inbound shipment and the "to" outbound shipment industries are on your layout.

You can use the phone book to find industry names and brands and an atlas to locate towns that might be near your railroad. You can have plenty of fun with just a single main town, with sidings around your layout as the other towns that ship or receive commodities via your railroad. Any part of any siding can be designated as a team track to accept just about anything, including oil or gas delivered to waiting tank trucks and trailers.

Make enough waybills so you have at least four for each of your freight cars. Prepare both sides of each of the waybill cards. First, write "to" on the upper right side

Here are some examples, each derived from the previous list of industries, to get you started:

INDUSTRY	TO	FROM
Milk	Station	Hoods Creamery, West Chester
Grain	Cargill Elevator	Western Co-op, Julesburg
Logs	Perkins Mill	Camp 14, Castle Creek
Coal	Blue Diamond Coal	Blue Diamond Tipple 12, Breton
Coal	Diamond Processing	Blue Diamond Tipple 12, Breton

of each waybill that ends with the sentence, "Place card in yard file." Next, write the name of the town on your layout where that industry is located, and the name of the industry. List the type of car that would be used for the commodity that the industry receives from that list of "in" commodities, then write "Empty for loading."

Turn the card over to the side that ends with the words "and file the waybill and packet in the Town set-out box." Write "to" at the top right of the card and pick one destination from your list of "to" places for that industry's products. If the commodity is coming from Chicago, write "From Chicago, via" and fill in the name of the town on your layout with the interchange, followed by the word *interchange*. If the commodity is coming from some town and industry that is actually on your layout, list that town and the industry below the word *to*. Below this, write the type of car, just as you did on the opposite side of the waybill, but here add the word *loaded* and write down the commodity the car will actually be carrying.

You should be able to make at least four of these cards, each with a different destination, for every industry on your layout. Remember, some industries might need two or more different types of cars, as well as different types of loads. A coal dealer might receive coal in bulk from hopper cars, but bagged coal in boxcars.

Make a clear plastic car packet for each car with clear plastic 2 1/4x3 1/2-inch envelopes. Place a 1/2x3/4-inch sticker in the upper left corner. Write the initials of the railroad marked on the car side, followed by the car number.

You will need an empty box to hold the cards and envelopes at the yard, the main operating point for your railroad. You also will want a box for every other town on the layout.

OPERATING THE WAYBILL SYSTEM

Spot at least one car at each town and put its clear plastic envelope with a waybill inside near the car (in the box marked with the town name). Put the rest of the cars in the yard for now, even if that means you make up a four-car train and park it by the yard sign. Put the car packets for those cars in that train in the box marked yard. Pick some waybills that match the cars, at random, from the pile you prepared and insert one in each of the cars in all the towns and in the yard into the car packets. For now, don't worry, which side of the waybill is up. The "up" for a car packet is the side on which you placed the sticker with the car number and description.

Follow the directions on the waybills and the system should run by itself. Keep the extra waybills in the yard file box, and when loose waybills are available, put them at the back of the pile. Pick a fresh waybill card each time you are ready to operate a train.

When the car is spotted at an industry, it can rest there for as long as you wish. The next train through can pick it up, or if you want a variation on the system, make a card that says," "Hold two days for unloading" on one side and "Hold one day for unloading" on the other side. The first train through turns the card over to the "one day" side, and the next train removes the card so the third train can pick up the empty (or loaded) car. Of course, if you are computer-literate, you can produce the cards on your computer and print them out to add a more "official" look to your waybill system.

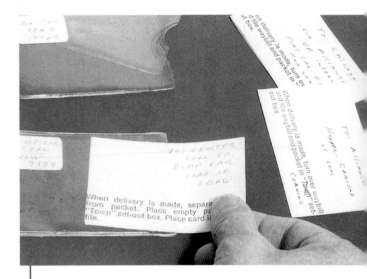

Use the 3/4x1/2-inc white stickers to mark the clear envelopes with the freight car railroad name and car number. To load a car, insert one of the waybills that represents an appropriate load the car would carry.

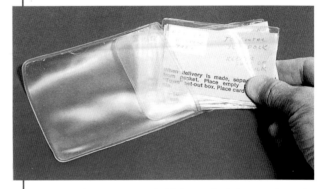

Use a pocket protector to hold the stack of clear envelopes for one train. The envelopes stay near the matching car wherever that car is spotted on the layout.

Chapter 16

STRUCTURES

Buildings and structures form the support system for Lionel trains. Structures are the railroad's connection with its customers and passengers, and they imply that this is not just a toy train but a miniature environment with living people at work and play.

LIGHTING YOUR LIONEL LAYOUT

Lighting adds a fourth dimension to the layout and suggests that real people are in the scene. The Lionelville series of businesses and homes includes interior lighting. Combined with the array of operating structures in the Lionel and American Flyer lines, your options are nearly limitless.

Lionel has always offered an assortment of outdoor lights ranging from city streetlights to highway lights, spotlights, and floodlight towers that can be used to light entire freight yards or miniature baseball parks.

Lionel has also created a variety of searchlight cars that can be an exciting addition to a night scene. There are several versions of the simple swiveling spotlight on a flatcar that can illuminate the layout as the train travels. The Lionel extension searchlight cars are depressed-center flatcars with a cable reel and a removable searchlight that can be used on the car or illuminate a nearby scene as long as the car is stationary. Lionel has also offered the somewhat more complex 3530 Electro Mobile power car with a simulated generator inside that is connected to a lighting pole and portable spotlight.

Robert Babas has installed lighting in all of the structures on his layout and provided a variety of street lights, floodlights, and illuminated locomotive cabs and passenger car interiors.

This highway scene cuts across the middle of Michael Ulewicz's layout. A mirror effectively doubles the length of this highway underpass scene.

The unusual 3530 Electro Mobile power car has a simulated generator inside with a portable spotlight that is connected to a lighting pole on Michael Ulewicz's layout.

Lionelville buildings and action accessories like the Lionel hobby shop have full interior lighting. The Walthers Palace Theater has operating running lights on Michael Ulewicz's layout.

BRINGING LIFE TO THE CITY

Lionel offers a range of action accessories that recreate the movement of people in a town or city. The Newsstand, with the news agent waving the paper he is selling, is a popular city scene accessory. Lionel has also offered a variety of Lionelville stores with full interiors and animation, like Harry's Barber Shop where the barbers move, the Lionel Hobby Shop, and others. There are more of these accessories in Chapter 17.

Lionel also offers rotating radar towers and the 465 Dispatching Station that features a loudspeaker inside to create your own broadcast or play back recorded messages.

The news agent in the Lionel 128 Newsstand appears to be handing a newspaper to his customer on Richard Kughn's layout.

The Lionel 465 Dispatching Station has a loudspeaker inside to record and broadcast messages. The microwave tower simulates the devices a real control tower might use to relay information on Michael Ulewicz's layout..

Michael Ulewicz grouped oil derricks and an oil-pumping station to create this oil industry scene. The oil tanks are HO scale models from Bachmann that have been repainted and lettered with decals.

The roundhouse on the Lionel Visitors Center layout is a cast-resin kit that has been painted and weathered.

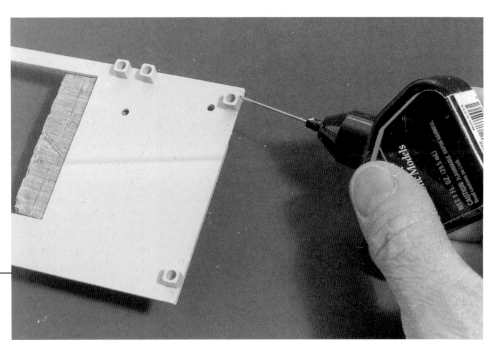

Use Testors Model Master cement for plastic models to assemble the injection-molded plastic kits.

Paint the windows, doors, and trim before installing them in the model. Fold masking tape into a loop, sticky side out, and stick the parts to the tape to hold them while you spray paint them with a can of flat finish.

PAINTING STRUCTURES

You may decide to customize your Lionelville buildings or operating accessory structures by painting them colors that match your unique layout environment.

WEATHERING STRUCTURES FOR REALISM

Real-world structures, like railroad locomotives and cars, quickly become dirty and the paint fades. Modelers call this natural process weathering, and you can replicate it effectively on your structures.

If you are going to apply decal signs to the structure, decide if you want them to be weathered or look freshly painted. If you want them to look weathered, apply the signs before you begin the weathering process.

You can simulate faded paint by mixing one part light gray acrylic or watercolor paint with nine parts water. Brush the mixture over the model and let it dry. If the paint still does not look faded enough, apply another coat or mix a stronger solution with one part paint to five parts water. You can apply subtle streaks down the roof to simulate rain-washed grime and oxidation. You can use this same mixture to highlight the mortar in brick or stone structures. Apply the mixture to one wall at a time and rest the brick or stone-walled model horizontally so the dilute light gray will puddle in the seams to create instant mortar.

Use dark brown or burnt umber in a similar diluted mixture to produce the dark streaks and blotches from smoke stains. This effect would be more pronounced on layout set in a time period prior to the 1950s when steam locomotives were active.

Finally, mix some brown or beige paint to match the color of the earth around the structure. Make a dilute mixture of this color and apply it around the base of the building where rain would splash mud onto the walls. You can also apply a diluted mixture to the walls and roof where dust would have washed down the surfaces.

These structures are all out-of-production Lionel kits including a shortened Rico Station, a passenger/freight station, and a freight platform.

Lionel called this kit the coaling station, but it was actually a replica of a mine tipple. Here it is being used to simulate a tipple loading Lionel ore cars on the Lionel Visitors Center layout.

A Lionel pumping station operates across the tracks from the oil company's supply shed on Larry LaJambe's layout. Larry repainted and weathered the Lionel freight platform.

This is a Lionel freight platform and operating switch tower on Michael Ulewicz's layout. The operating switch tower has been offered in several colors over the years. The tower man moves out onto the platform when the operating button is pushed.

Michael Ulewicz assembled this Lionel grain elevator, then weathered it with a dilute mixture of nine parts water to one part burnt umber.

Larry LaJambe painted and weathered his Lionel grain elevator. Note the rust streaks on the lean-to's roof.

This Lionel passenger/freight station kit was assembled, painted, and weathered by Larry LaJambe.

Michael Ulewicz used two Lionel Rico Station kits to create this long depot. He cut the freight station from one of the kits, turned it front-to-back, and installed it on the opposite end of the station.

You can custom fit the plastic kits by trimming the walls and roof to the size you wish with a razor saw. Use a piece of masking tape to help guide the cut. (Adults only please).

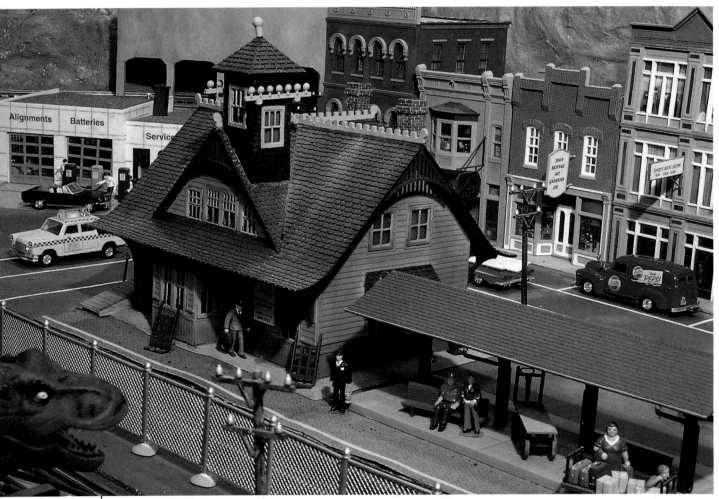

The Lionel Rico Station kit, painted in an ornate turn-of-the-century style, is weathered and featured on Larry LaJambe's layout.

Chapter 17

ACTION ACCESSORIES

The trains on our Lionel layouts certainly provide plenty of action. But there's a lot more activity going on in the real world than just trains, and you can duplicate much of that action with Lionel accessories.

In the real world, buildings are illuminated and street and flood lights are turned on as the sun goes down. Oil and gas wells pump 24/7. Some industries are busy loading crates, coal, lumber, logs, barrels, scrap steel, ice, and other commodities into railroad cars and other industries are busy unloading similar commodities. All of that action and more is available to provide a level of realism and excitement that is only possible with Lionel.

YOUR CHOICE OF ACTION

The most popular Lionel accessories are those that duplicate the action of a real industry, such as the log

Michael Ulewicz has included examples of most of Lionel's lights and illuminated structures, such as the 192 railroad control tower, operating signals with glowing red or green lights, and crossing warning gates with flashing red lights.

The most exciting Lionel layouts have groups of action accessories like the American Flyer oil-drum loader, pipe company, American Flyer sawmill, and No. 397 operating coal loader on Robert Babas' layout.

Most Lionel railroaders group as many action accessories as they can on parallel tracks. Robert Babas has the unloading platform for a Lionel operating milk car opposite the log bin on the Lionel log loader. The cattle pen for the operating cattle car is to the left.

The Lionel No. 464R operating sawmill simulates the action of a massive saw blade slicing through logs and moving them out on the overhead conveyor.

loader. Lionel has made a variety of action accessories to recreate the action of the coal, lumber, milk, and steel industries, as well as variety of freight-handling industries that move barrels, concrete pipes, and complete intermodal containers or trailers. Some of the real-world industries that ship and receive commodities by rail are described in Chapter 15.

Lionel accessories also recreate the action of oil and gas industry facilities. The Lionel oil derrick simulates the pumping action of a real oil well, the oil field with bubbling tubes simulates oil bubbling though clear pipes.

From oil pumping to the action of a complete locomotive servicing facility, these are extremes of the array of Lionel action accessories. The three-piece Steam

This Shell Oil derrick on the Lionel Visitors Center layout will pump out crude 24/7, just like the real derricks.

The Steam Clean and Wheel Grinder units were introduced in 1991, 1993, and 1995.

Clean & Wheel-Grinding Shop was only produced in 1991, 1993, and 1995. This structure simulates the wheel-grinding, train-washing, and steam-cleaning facilities of real railroads. As the train rolls through the gantry, simulated sparks fly as the wheels are ground round once more, the brushes spin to wash the train, and the steam-cleaning facility points its smoking nozzles at the cars and locomotives.

ANIMATED CITIES

Some of the most interesting Lionel accessories don't load or unload anything. Lionelville features an ever-growing

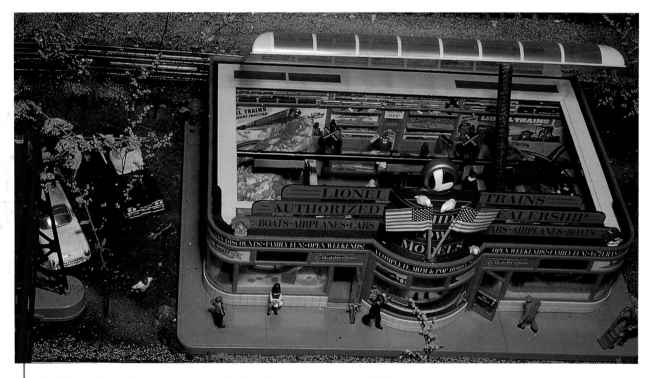

The Midtown Hobby Shop recreates a massive Lionel train store, complete with three operating layouts.

You would expect that Richard Kughn, who is part-owner of Lionel, would have one of the Lionel factory buildings on his layout.

Lionel has offered several different colored lighthouses, each with rotating beacon and foghorn, such as this one on Richard Kughn's layout.

variety of animated city structures, including a hobby shop, aquarium, car dealership, and an amusement park with merry-go-round, Ferris wheel, shooting gallery, and a host of other rides and attractions. A series of businesses and houses in the Lionelville line have also been introduced.

One of the most fascinating Lionel action accessories is the Lionel Hobby Shop. This is a replica of a large hobby shop with clear skylights and huge picture windows so you can see what's going on inside. There's full interior detail with 1/48-scale replicas of Lionel trains actually running around three operating layouts. The Lionelville Ford Dealership is housed in a similar building, but three "new" Fords from the 1950s rotate on display tables inside the business.

Within recent Lionel lines are resurrected models of two of the most sought-after tinplate models of the 1930s, the Lionel factory and the 849 industrial power station from 1928.

Some of the structures from the waterfront areas of major cities, including a lighthouse, complete with rotating beacon and foghorn sound are also offered.

Lionel has produced several tugboats like those used by real railroads to push car floats loaded with freight cars across the Hudson River and other major waterways. The Baltimore & Ohio, New York Central, Santa Fe, and Pennsylvania tugboats have interior lighting, a realistic whistle, and an operating smokestack.

OPERATING THE ACTION ACCESSORIES

Any Lionel action accessory can be powered with current from the same transformer used to control the trains. In fact, most Lionel transformers have an additional pair of posts designed to provide the current needed for accessories. Accessories can, however, slow down the trains as they draw the current to light up, load, or unload a car. It's wise to purchase a separate transformer just for accessories. Each action accessory is furnished with its own remote-control operating box on an electrical cable. You may, however, also want to purchase the special loading or unloading freight cars that are used with specific accessories.

OPERATING ACCESSORIES WITH TRAINMASTER

You can operate most Lionel action accessories with the O and O-27 or FasTrack buttons remote-control tracks, which can also be activated by pushing a single button on the TrainMaster CAB-1 Remote Controller. You will need a operating track controller (OTC) or SC-2. In order to make this activation truly "remote controlled"

The door on this operating gateman is ajar even when the accessory is turned off. The door can be adjusted from beneath the platform.

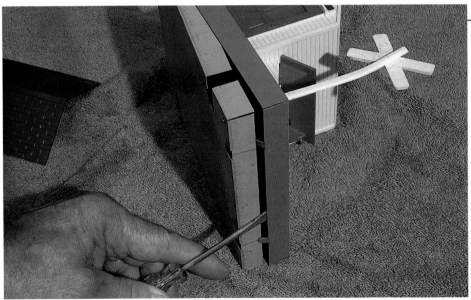

Gently pry the two metal tabs on the platform's base upward about 3/4 inch, then use a screwdriver to pry the edge of the platform out to clear the tabs. The bent (and backwards) crossbuck can also be replaced.

from anywhere on your layout, each OTC will operate two remote-control track sections or four uncoupling track sections.

REPAIRING LIONEL ACTION ACCESSORIES

Each Lionel action accessory has been designed for decades of trouble-free operation. Many have been tested by both the factory Quality Control Team and thousands of satisfied consumers for over half a century. Action accessories should be cleaned periodically and the mechanism examined for any grit or lint that may inhibit their operation. Clean the mechanism just as you would a locomotive, by appling a drop of oil to each

bearing and a trace of grease to each gear tooth. Always try to avoid over lubrication, which can be as bad for an accessory as under lubrication. If repairs are required, contact an authorized Lionel Service Station or the Lionel Service Center in Chesterfield, Michigan, at 586-949-4100 ext. 1360.

REPAIRING THE AUTOMATIC GATEMAN

Many Lionel layouts include the out-of-scale Automatic Gateman, one of the most popular Lionel accessories of the past century. The first Automatic Gateman was introduced in 1935 and is still an important part of the Lionel line. The earliest crossing gateman (from 1935 to 1949) had a stamped-metal base, shanty, pole and crossbuck, and a cast-metal figure. In 1950, the shanty was replaced with a more detailed plastic shed with a plastic pole and crossbuck. The all-metal operating gateman activated with a pair of levers.

The Automatic Gateman that has been produced for the past 50 years operates on a rack and pinion system. The rack (a quarter-circle with gear teeth) that moves the gateman out the door drives a spur gear or pinion, which opens the door. The accessory is activated by a 153C contactor, an insulated track section, or a 153IR controller. A solenoid is powered in the base of the crossing gateman, which moves its plunger outward to push the rack to move the gateman out the door.

If the gateman does not work at all, go through the steps in the troubleshooting chart in this chapter. If the Automatic Gateman only gets halfway out the door or if the door fails to close, the door's spur gear may have jumped a tooth or two on the gateman's spur gear. To reset the gears, remove the base. The gray metal base is held to the green metal foundation with metal tabs.

We watched as Chuck Sartor, the service technician for Mizell Trains, an authorized Lionel repair station, repaired a crossing gateman. The trick to preserving the tabs is to bend them only about halfway up—just a bit beyond 90 degrees. Bending them straight weakens and eventually tears the metal. Move the edge of the base out far enough to disengage one tab, then repeat the process with the other tab. With the base removed, you can gently move the geared rack up enough to engage other teeth on the door's spur or pinion gear. Work the lever manually and move the rack a tooth at a time until you get the action just right. Check to be sure that the rack is not permanently bent so it can skip a tooth during operation, and if necessary, rebend it. This is a good time to clean all the working parts and apply new grease. If the crossbuck's pole is bent or broken, you can obtain a replacement from your authorized Lionel Service Station or directly from the Lionel National Service Center in Chesterfield, Michigan; calling 1-800-4LIONEL; or by visiting the Lionel website at www.lionel.com.

With the base removed, you can pull up on the steel gear rack to engage the proper teeth on the round pinion (spur) gear to synchronize the door closing with the gateman at rest.

Troubleshooting Operating Accessories

Symptom: Accessory does not operate

1. If the accessory is wired to the track or the track posts on the transformer, the transformer speed control must be nearly on full to operate the accessory. This is one reason why I recommend that accessories be powered by a separate transformer.
2. Check the wire connections at both the controller and the power to the accessory.
3. Try operating any mechanical accessories by hand to determine if the components might be jammed.
4. Try operating the accessory on a brief jolt of 18 volts to see if that frees the mechanism. Try a quick dozen bursts of power, but do not, under any circumstances, leave the power on in the hope that prolonged power will free the accessory—it will burn out the motor or solenoid.
5. On log loaders, be sure to use only the special round-wood dowels that Lionel supplies with the log-dump cars or the accessory packs of logs. Regular sticks or the rough logs supplied with some non-dumping log cars will jam the log loader.
6. On coal loaders, use only the coal Lionel supplies for the accessory. Other types of "coal," sand, or other granular substances can jam the coal-loading accessory mechanisms.

GLOSSARY

AAR: The Association of American Railroads; the organization of real railroads that established standards for couplers, other mechanical components, and in some cases, designs for complete cars.

Articulated: A steam locomotive with two sets of driving wheels. One set is pivoted to allow the locomotive to negotiate tighter curves without derailing.

Bad order: A term used to identify a freight car that needs to be repaired before it can be placed back into revenue service.

Big hook: The wrecking crane that uses its boom, cables, and hooks to rerail cars and locomotives.

Block: An electrically isolated section of track needed to operate two or more trains at once with conventional control. It is also a group or set of two or more cars heading for the same destination.

Branchline: A lesser-used portion of a real railroad that may lead to smaller towns or specific industries located away from the mainline.

CTC: centralized traffic control. It's also another historical name for Lionel's track-connecting Lockon.

Controller: A box with levers used to control the trains' speed and direction. It may also include buttons to control sounds or other devices. Also, Lionel offers a special train-warning trigger device called a 153IR Controller.

Contactor: A Lionel 153C Contactor Switch is placed beneath the rails to actuate signals or other warning devices. It is triggered by the weight of passing trains.

Crossover: The X-shaped place where two tracks cross each other on a figure 8 layout or at the junction of two railroads. Also, the place where a pair of parallel tracks, such as a double-track mainline, are connected by two switches so trains can move from one mainline track to the other.

Cut: A ditch through a hill to maintain a level railroad path across the countryside. See also *Fill.*

Draft gear: The components that support the coupler on cars and locomotives. Usually, the draft gear will also incorporate some type of spring or other cushioning device to lessen the impact of cars being coupled or stopped too quickly.

Fill: An earthen embankment to support the tracks above valleys or minor depressions and maintain a level path across the countryside. See also *Cut.*

Flange: The largest diameter portion of a railroad wheel or locomotive driver that keeps the wheel on the rail.

Frog: The place where the two rails cross at a switch or crossing.

Gap: The electrically isolated point on the rail where a fiber pin is used in place of a steel pin.

Gauge: The distance between the tops of the rails. On American railroads, the standard gauge is 4 feet, 8 1/2 inches between the tops of the rails. See also *Narrow gauge.*

Grade: The uphill and downhill portions of a railroad.

Grabiron: The steel handles on the sides of cars and locomotives to help workers climb onto the sides or roof.

Head end cars: The baggage, mail, and express cars between the rear of the locomotive and the first of the passenger cars.

Helper: An additional locomotive that is added to a train to provide extra power to get the train over a steep grade. Helpers are usually placed at the rear of the train where they can be uncoupled quickly, although sometimes helpers are placed mid-train or at the front of the train.

Hi-rail: The term used to describe model railroads that are built with exact-scale cars and locomotives and three-rail track. Since the rails are proportionally larger than exact-scale, they are high.

Hostler: The worker who moves locomotives to fill them with fuel, water, and sand or places them in storage or repair shops.

Hotbox: When a bearing on the end of an axle becomes overheated.

Interchange: The places on a real railroad where connections are made with adjoining railroads so individual cars or complete trains can be transferred from one railroad to another.

Interlocking: A system of mechanical levers or electronic devices used to move switches and signals so the signals show the proper route for each train to prevent derailments.

Intermodal: Using two or more means of transportation for the same load. Containers are often loaded onto a truck to be transferred to an open railroad car to be carried to a dock area where a crane will transfer them to a ship. The term is also used to describe intermodal cars, cranes, and terminals.

Journal: The bearing that supports the end of a railroad car or locomotive axle.

Kingpin: The pivot point for a freight or passenger car truck where it connects to the bolster.

LCL: Less-than-carload lot shipments that are too small to fill a freight car.

Lockon: The fiber plate with metal wire clips to connect the electrical power to Lionel O and O-27 three-rail track.

Mainline: The primary track the real railroad dedicates to the most important passenger and freight trains; the track or tracks that run cross-country. It is also Lionel's brand name for the series of more scale dimensioned and crossing-warning devices.

Maintenance-of-way: Freight cars or rail vehicles directly associated with maintaining the railroad or repairing and righting wrecked trains.

Narrow gauge: Some early American railroads and industrial railroads that served logging camps or mining districts were built to a 3-foot gauge and some were built to a 2-foot gauge. The smaller gauges are referred to as narrow gauge. See also *Gauge*.

Peddler freight: A freight train designated to switch cars at most towns along its route from terminal to terminal. Also called way freight.

Piggyback: An early term used for special flatcar service to transport highway trailers. Also called TOFC (trailers on flatcars). See also *Intermodal*.

Points: The portions of a switch that move to change the track's route from the mainline to a siding.

Prototype: The term used to describe the full-size car, locomotive, or structure that a model is supposed to duplicate.

Pullman: The passenger cars that were owned and operated by the Pullman Company, usually sleeping cars, diners, or parlor cars. Term is also used to describe any sleeping car.

Reefer: Freight cars cooled by either ice in bunkers fed through hatches on the roof or by mechanical refrigeration units.

Right of way: Land and track owned by the railroad.

Spot: When a car is moved to its desired position on the track, usually beside some industry's loading platform.

Switch: A term used by model railroaders to refer to the portion of the railroad track that allows the trains to change routes. Term is also used for electrical switches on model railroads, such as on-off switches. Real railroads often call track switches turnouts to avoid this confusion. Term is also used to describe a locomotive picking up and dropping off cars.

Tank engine: A steam locomotive that carries the coal or fuel oil in a bunker behind the cab and the water in a tank over the top of the boiler. There is no need for separate tender to carry fuel or water.

Tender: The car that carries fuel and water. It is coupled just behind most steam locomotives.

Throat: The area where yard trackage begins to diverge into multiple tracks for storage and switching.

Timetable: The document that tells when trains are scheduled to be at certain stations or points on the railroad.

TMCC: Lionel's TrainMaster Command Control system is described in Chapters 6 and 7.

Turnout: See *Switch*.

Trolley: Self-propelled electric-powered cars that operated almost exclusively on city streets.

Truck: The frame and four (or more) wheels under each end of most railroad freight and passenger cars.

Turntable: A rotating bridge to turn locomotives or cars in the engine or roundhouse.

Vestibule: The enclosed area, usually at both ends of a passenger car, where passengers enter the car from the station platform and can walk from one car to the next.

Way freight: See *Peddler freight*.

Wye: A track switch where both routes curve away in opposite directions from the single straight track. It's also the triangular-shaped track (in plan view) where trains can be reversed.

RESOURCES

There are hundreds of suppliers of model railroad products, but very few sell direct to consumers. You can order any of the brands mentioned in this book from your authorized Lionel dealer or you may be able to locate other shops that sell model railroad items by looking under "Model and Construction Supplies, Retail" in the telephone book. You can find the name of the nearest authorized Lionel dealer or authorized service center by calling 1-800-454-6635 or by looking on the Lionel Website: www.lionel.com.

LIONEL RESTORATION AND REPRODUCTION PARTS AND SERVICES

The Lionel Customer Service Department can supply many parts for older trains. Your dealer can contact Lionel for you, or you can go to www.lionel.com, and look under "Customer Service" on the homepage.

CLUBS AND ORGANIZATIONS

Lionel Railroader Club (LRRC)
P. O. Box 748
New Baltimore, MI 48047
(586) 949-4100
www.lionel.com/clubs/lrrc

Train Collectors Association (TCA)
P.O. Box 248
Strasburg, PA 17579-0248
www.traincollectors.org

Lionel Collectors Club of America (LCCA)
Business Office
P.O. Box 479
LaSalle, IL 61301-0479
www.lionelcollectors.org

Lionel Operating Train Society (LOTS)
Business Office
6376 West Fork Road
Cincinatti, OH 45247-5704
www.lots-trains.org

Toy Train Operating Society (TTOS)
25 W. Walnut Street, Suite 308
Pasadena, CA 91103
www.ttos.org

PUBLICATIONS

Inside Track
Lionel Railroader Club
P. O. Box 748
New Baltimore, MI 48047
(586) 949-4100
www.lionel.com/club/lrrc

Classic Toy Trains
Kalmbach Publishing
P. O. Box 1612
Waukesha, WI 53187
(800) 533-6644
www.classictoytrains.com

O Gauge Railroader
OGR Publishing
33 Sheridan Road, Suite 2
Youngstown, OH 44514

INDEX

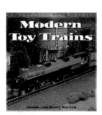